MINDS

OVER

MEETINGS

MINDS

A Personal Perspective on

OVER

Wellness in the Workplace

MEETINGS

KODY
GREEN

WILEY

For general information on our other products and services or for technical support, please contact our Customer Care Department within the United States at (800) 762-2974, outside the United States at (317) 572-3993 or fax (317) 572-4002.

Wiley also publishes its books in a variety of electronic formats. Some content that appears in print may not be available in electronic formats. For more information about Wiley products, visit our web site at www.wiley.com.

Library of Congress Cataloging-in-Publication Data is Available

ISBN: 9781394289592 (Cloth)
ISBN: 9781394289608 (ePub)
ISBN: 9781394289585 (ePDF)

Cover Design: Wiley
Cover Image: © marozhkastudio/Adobe Stock
Author Photo: © Kody Green

SKY10090313_110824

To Mom, for always being there to teach me about life, work, or mental health, even when she struggled to care for herself.

Contents

Preface

Hello, my name is Kody Green (he/him), and I had my first symptoms of psychosis and a psychotic break at 18, which led to me dropping out of college, losing my job, and falling into addiction. I struggled for more than two years undiagnosed and in active addiction. After being incarcerated for charges related to my addiction, I received a diagnosis of schizophrenia, which also led to battles with mental health issues like increased stress, anxiety, and depression.

After I became stable with the help of medication and treatment, I worked at various jobs – but always hid my illness while having setbacks and then either losing my job or moving on before they could fire me. It wasn't until I had a breakthrough conversation with an HR manager, which I'll tell you about in Chapter 1, that I started down the path I am on today.

Currently, I am a motivational speaker, mental health advocate, and content creator with almost two million followers across social media platforms. I started making content about schizophrenia and mental health awareness in 2019, when I was pursuing a degree in HR management hoping to advocate for employees struggling with mental health or mental illness. I wanted to use social media to spread awareness about these topics by sharing stories of my own experiences with schizophrenia and mental health issues.

Soon after the COVID-19 pandemic hit, my social media following ballooned to more than one million followers. There was a huge influx of people seeking content about mental health because of the pandemic. The pandemic caused many people to have to start addressing mental health and acknowledging how difficult major life events can be. Isolation can be difficult for anyone and can have detrimental impacts on a person's mental health. People were having to learn to cope with this ongoing isolation, loss, and situational uncertainty. I was speaking all over the country at colleges, conventions, and workplaces talking about mental health, overcoming addiction, and embracing the need for mental health awareness at work.

I've talked to people who have shared their diagnoses and employment experiences with me, I've talked to employers who wanted to know how they could provide support, and I've talked to people who wanted to help their coworkers that may be struggling with mental health. It's all these conversations that made me want to continue helping people better understand mental health in the workplace – by writing this book.

Specifically, in Part I, "Introduction to Mental Health in the Workplace," I'll talk more about my background, the difference between *mental health* and *mental illness,* and

addressing misconceptions about mental health at work.
In addition to being a person living with a serious mental
illness and ongoing mental health struggles, I have worked
in a wide variety of different types of jobs and industries.
I grew up understanding the importance of a good work
ethic but recognized later in life that I may not be able to
perform like everyone else because of my mental health
needs.

In Part II of this book, "Being on the Job with Mental
Health Issues," we get at the heart of the issue: how to
handle working at a job if you have mental health issues.
Should you tell your boss? What accommodations are
required by law? How do you set boundaries? How do you
recognize the signs of burning out? What does self-care
look like during the 9-to-5 grind? I'll answer all these
questions and more, all while sharing what worked for
me. I'll also introduce you to others who have firsthand
experience of the realities of being on the job with mental
health issues.

In Part III, "Supporting Employees with Mental Health
Issues," I'll talk about antiquated workplace policies that
I hope you aren't seeing at your job, as well as how
employers can rebuild workplace culture into a modern
reality. I'll also talk about management and coworkers'
roles for people with mental health issues thriving while
on the job. While speaking with employers about mental
health in the workplace over the last several years,
I have been able to see what has worked well to retain
employees and also what some companies have done

poorly that has caused incredibly high turnover rates. Some companies are leading the changes in workplace culture and seeing the positive result from investing in mental health resources; however, we still have a long way to go. I end the book with my hopes for the future and resources for where you can go from here.

Part I

Introduction to Mental Health in the Workplace

Chapter 1

All About Me and My Diagnosis

I remember the embarrassment and humiliation I felt having to look my human resources manager in the eyes and explain to her that I had a diagnosis of schizophrenia. I also had to disclose that I had ongoing struggles with several other mental health issues, and I didn't know what to expect. I had known for a while about my diagnosis, and I had not told my previous employers because I was afraid of being judged by my coworkers or discriminated against. I had been working at this company for a full year, and I also had not told any of my coworkers or my manager.

I knew that my coworkers suspected something, as I had overheard another employee say that he could tell that "something was wrong" with me. Although I was on medication that reduced my schizophrenia symptoms, I still · had breakthrough symptoms like auditory and visual hallucinations and many unresolved mental health issues like depression and anxiety as a result of my diagnosis.

I was too afraid to talk about my mental health because I knew what people thought about individuals living with mental health issues. I lived in a small, rural community, and people often spoke very poorly about the very idea of mental health issues. They would say things like:

- "I wouldn't let my kid go to therapy. That's not how our family deals with things."
- "Who cares if you are sad? Pull yourself up by your bootstraps and get over it!"
- "People who need medication are just weak."

I figured that I was doing just fine since I had managed to hold on to this job and that I just had more issues with stress and anxiety than most people. I figured that is what made it harder for me to function day to day. I was under the impression that my poor mental health was somehow my fault and that I just needed to work harder like everyone else. But every time I tried to ignore my mental health issues, I would end up in burnout, and that is how I had lost jobs in the past.

When I started having symptoms of mental illness, my coworkers and even my direct manager at my previous jobs would eventually notice that something wasn't quite right with me, and it usually ended with me feeling forced out or being fired. I did tell some employers in job interviews that I had occasional mental health struggles that I was working through, but I would never get a call back. When I did manage to get jobs, some of my coworkers would find out about my struggles because no matter how hard I tried, I could not hide my mental health issues or mental illness forever.

I could pretend I was fine for a while and even do an amazing job and outperform my coworkers, but it always led to burnout, and it wasn't sustainable. In this particular role – I was working as a distribution center operator at a food manufacturing company – I was struggling to perform and was having issues with attendance, so I knew that I would eventually have to tell human resources if I wanted to keep my job, but I was terrified to do it.

When I finally decided to have the conversation, my HR manager's reaction to the news was not what I was expecting. She simply looked at me and said, "I am sorry to hear about your diagnosis and the status of your mental health. That must be incredibly difficult. Do you have any reasonable accommodations you need from us?" Then she started to fill me in about the company's options for accommodations, resources, and assistance to ensure that I could continue to work there.

I couldn't believe that she responded in a way that seemed so supportive and encouraging. She even told me about the company's employee assistance program (EAP) and mental health resources and helped me apply for the Family and Medical Leave Act (FMLA) to ensure that I didn't lose my job if I needed to miss days for appointments or take days off when I was struggling.

I know this may sound ridiculous, but I was expecting the HR folks to say that I couldn't work there anymore. I had always been told that people with mental health issues or diagnosed mental illnesses were "crazy" and incapable of working or maintaining a normal lifestyle. I was so afraid of anyone knowing that I struggled with mental health issues that I drove myself to exhaustion just trying to hide it. I didn't want to admit that I ever struggled with depression or symptoms like paranoia and hallucinations, especially to my employer.

Besides losing jobs because of not knowing how to discuss my mental health with employers, I was also discouraged to discuss my mental health because I had seen other people I knew lose jobs due to issues with mental health, including my own mother.

I was raised by a single mother who was diagnosed with schizoaffective disorder when I was in high school. She went from working three jobs to support her kids to being unemployed and on disability because her mental illness and her issues maintaining positive mental health made it impossible for her to keep a job no matter how hard she tried. She was always the hardest worker I knew, and suddenly she was struggling with such severe depression and psychosis that I had to become a full-time caregiver as a teenager. It was so confusing and devastating to watch the most driven and hardworking person I knew not be able to even get out of bed or bathe herself. My mother was my first introduction to what mental health and mental illness truly looked like.

When I developed schizophrenia symptoms in college, I figured that I would never be able to work again. I assumed that I would have to go on disability, like my mom. Despite wanting to work when I got stable on medication and wanting to have a better and more comfortable life,

I figured that my condition and my constant mental health symptoms would make it impossible.

I had been convinced that it would be unlikely that I would ever get to a point of stability or cognitive function that would allow me to be anywhere near where I was before my psychotic break, especially after a doctor told me that due to the severity of my mental illness and my constant mental health afflictions that I should just plan on being unemployed because there was "no way" I would be able to get or hold a job. Yes, a doctor said that. And I believed it. Getting a mental-health diagnosis was already so confusing and scary, but being told I would be disabled for the rest of my life was devastating.

One of the reasons I believed that people with a similar illness as I have could never work or be successful was because all I had ever known about people with schizophrenia or mental illness is what I saw on TV shows, movies, and media, all of which portrayed people with mental illness in a very negative light. The only person I had ever met with a similar diagnosis was my mom, and due to many years without treatment, her symptoms manifested differently for her than mine did for me in my own experience.

Unfortunately, my mom went almost a decade undiagnosed (or with incorrect diagnoses) with no resources or medication, and it had irreversible cognitive effects. Although she is doing better now and has regained some cognitive function, I watched my mother struggle to survive as we couldn't afford basic necessities with her being on disability. Both my siblings and I were forced to care for our mom at a young age as well as start working while still in high school to pay for basic necessities.

I knew my mom's inability to work was out of her control, but I knew I wanted to work as an adult. Of course, I didn't think I would have similar mental health issues in my adult life.

Years after my initial mental health episodes, I got somewhat stable from medication and treatment. The more stable I got, the more I felt the need to prove that I could not only work but thrive in both my personal and professional lives. I think that is why having to tell my employer about all of the mental health issues I was dealing with felt especially embarrassing at the time.

I know now that I had no reason to be embarrassed about my diagnosis or my various mental health troubles, nor should I have been ashamed of having to tell someone else, but having been raised in a small, rural town in the Midwest, where people were proud of job longevity and company loyalty, I wasn't looking forward to having to quit my job or getting fired. From a very young age, I remember my grandfather constantly stressing the need for me to get a steady job and plan on staying there forever. He was a lifelong electrician and retired from the same company that he apprenticed with. In fact, he was another incredible hardworking person in my life; both my mom and my grandfather shaped my work ethic and were reasons why I pushed myself so hard when I reentered the workforce, usually working myself into burnout and worsening my mental health.

Still, my grandpa's employment journey was common for many of the people I knew in my hometown. They found jobs and stayed there for life, regardless of how the company may have mistreated them or underpaid them or how the job may have led to stress that affected their mental health and life outside of work. These were the types of work-place cultures that were similar to the first jobs I had in production, manufacturing, retail, and the service industry, and it became obvious that these companies and organizations cared very little about addressing mental health or even acknowledging it.

Another issue with growing up and working in a small rural town was it made it difficult for me to understand how common mental health issues and mental illnesses really are. No one talked about mental health in my home-town or in my family. Even after my mom was diagnosed, many of my family members refused to acknowledge or address it. That is why when I did start having mental health issues, I felt like it was a moral failing or like it was somehow my fault. I felt so alone, and I just wanted to be like everyone else who was able to work 40 hours, take care of their families, and take care of their home lives, but there were days and weeks that I couldn't even get out of bed or get through work each day, let alone worry about my responsibilities outside of work. I realized that if there was to be any chance of keeping my job, I needed to explain my situation to my employer, and that is why I brought it to my HR manager that day.

All About Me and My Diagnosis

After telling the HR manager about my diagnosis, I was so impressed with how it was handled that I even had a conversation with my direct manager, as recommended by the HR manager. I was hesitant at first, but the HR manager explained that disclosing my mental health issues and my schizophrenia diagnosis to my manager may make it easier for me to ask for help during my shifts, to start pursuing workplace accommodations, or even to look for other roles in the company if my mental health issues made me unable to continue to perform my job responsibilities.

I had a decent working relationship with my direct manager, but once again, I couldn't believe how reassuring the conversation was. He followed up with me to ensure that I knew what resources were available and to verify that HR had given me all information I needed. I found out years later that he knew about my struggles before I reached out, and he was just glad that I finally asked for help.

I felt so supported by this particular company and by its management, which I know from years of advocacy and working many jobs is not usually the case when people try to open up about their mental health or disclose a diagnosis with a manager. This job gave me the initial stability that I needed, and the support from management and human resources allowed me to stay with the company longer than I had ever been able to keep a job prior. This company not only acknowledged my mental health concerns but also accommodated me in every way they could. By taking my mental health and personal life into consideration, I felt safer and more comfortable, which allowed me to perform with more consistency, engagement, and excitement than ever before.

Unfortunately, I had plenty of other negative workplace experiences both before and after this story. I have also spoken with mental health advocates and patients all over the country who have expressed how rare positive workplace cultures are in most industries today. Most of the stories of mental health or mental illness in the workplace that I heard from advocates and peers were either addressed unprofessionally by leaders or ended negatively for the employee.

Most people are too afraid to have these conversations at work because they've either lost jobs or been treated differently after disclosing their mental health status, so they stopped reaching out for help the next time around. Being accommodated at work should be the norm! Everyone wants to be able to live comfortably, and having a good job can make that possible. However, keeping a "good job" can be very difficult when you are unable to function day to day due to severe anxiety, depression, or other mental health struggles. Although mental health awareness seems to be on the rise, conversations about mental health and mental illness in the context of the workplace still seem to be avoided. But ignoring it does not make the problems go away.

Mental health in the workplace is such an important topic because mental illness and mental health can affect anyone, at any time, without warning. In fact, I lived the first 18 years of my life without any symptoms or major mental health issues. If you had asked me, I would have considered myself "normal" for my entire adolescence. It wasn't until my first year of college that I experienced my first symptoms of psychosis and had a psychotic break. I was 21 years old by the time I received my diagnosis of schizophrenia, which caused new mental health issues like increased stress, anxiety, and depression.

When I finally got stable with medication and tried to get back to working, it was difficult to get a job and almost impossible to hold one consistently with my constant mental health issues. I saw my mother have the same difficulties during my adolescence and into my adult life, and although I felt terrible for her, at the time I thought, *That could never happen to me.* That is when I learned that mental illness can affect anyone.

So, after being at that job in which the HR team was so accommodating longer than I had worked anywhere else, I was inspired to go back to college (having dropped out during my psychotic break several years prior) to pursue a degree in HR management; I wanted to make a difference in the HR field and be a vocal advocate for workers struggling with mental health or mental illness.

How Work Has Affected Employee Mental Health

According to a 2024 National Alliance on Mental Illness (NAMI) poll,[1] one in three employees say their mental

[1]https://www.nami.org/support-education/publications-reports/survey-reports/the-2024-nami-workplace-mental-health-poll

health has suffered because of work in the past year. (This doesn't include individuals who struggle with mental health issues that pertain to their home lives, just those who are finding their job directly having a negative effect on their mental health.)

This shows not only the need to address how work can affect mental health in a negative way but also why employers need to work hard to ensure that their employees don't become part of this statistic. I have seen both personally and professionally how negative mental health can impact someone's ability to perform, engage, and succeed with the work they do.

Mental health has become a trending topic ever since the COVID-19 pandemic, which is a great thing, but we need to make sure that conversations are focused on more than just hashtags. It is also important to make sure that mental illness continues to be a part of the conversation. Many people who have mental illness don't recognize they have it until it has already had detrimental effects on their lives. Or, they may mistake mental illness for temporary mental health issues. Understanding the difference between the two can be an important part of understanding the needs of workers and how employers can be more prepared to help employees find proper resources. We'll talk about the difference between the two in the next chapter.

Chapter 2

Mental Health Versus Mental Illness
What Is the Difference?

Many people in America live with a mental illness, and many more people struggle with mental health issues. But what is the difference? If you ask the average American, you will probably find that they are not even aware that there is a difference between the two.

Some Definitions for You

Every single person has mental *health*, and everyone can experience issues with their mental health, with feelings of sadness, depression, anxiety, stress, and more. Mental health refers to a person's general well-being and their ability to cope with the stress of everyday life experiences. Mental health can affect everyone and can change throughout life based on situational occurrences.

Mental *illness*, on the other hand, is often a lifelong chronic disorder that requires early intervention, medication, and ongoing treatment. Examples of these disorders are bipolar disorder, major depression, generalized anxiety, schizophrenia, and dissociated identity disorder.

Mental health is always there and may be positive or negative, while mental illness is a diagnosable illness that affects a person's day-to-day capabilities for a long period of time.

Why Knowing the Difference Is Important

Many people will experience mental health issues while in the workplace. Work can increase stress and anxiety even if a person loves their job and the company they work for, so understanding the difference between mental health and mental illness can help employees manage their mental health, and it can help them understand when they may need to seek help for a more chronic condition. In addition, employers need to learn which resources may be better for different situations.

NAMI estimates that one in five adults in America experiences a mental illness.[1] Even if you are not directly affected by mental illness, chances are you know someone who is. The fact that 20% of adults have a diagnosable mental illness (and many more struggle with negative mental health issues) but no one talks about it (especially not at work) is shocking. That is why I am sharing my own story in the hopes of having an impact on society, individuals, and the workplace.

---

[1]https://www.nami.org/about-mental-illness/mental-health-conditions

As someone who has worked in many different industries, some before my diagnosis, I know that stress and other mental health ailments can be inevitable without proper self-care, something we'll talk about in Chapter 8. Most workplaces often require lots of change, rapid-fire decision-making, and fast-paced environments. This, with the addition of having to build and maintain working relationships with people you might barely know, can create a lot of conflicts and stressful situations.

Poor mental health can also be a result of life outside of work – relationship troubles, family obligations, or money woes – and it can be hard to "leave your problems at the door" when you arrive to work your shift. Working with stressful deadlines or spending more time on the job than with your own family can make poor mental health worse.

Communicating the difference between mental health and mental illness will make it easier for employers, HR, and coworkers to help individuals thrive in the workplace. When I started experiencing negative mental health symptoms, I did not realize that they were tied to an undiagnosed mental illness, so the assistance and resources that I was able to find were only temporary fixes for an unidentified, underlying, long-term issue. This can be the case for many people who start experiencing stress, anxiety, or depression symptoms that they believe are temporary or situational. Many may not realize that these issues can sometimes be a result of mental illness diagnoses (like schizophrenia, bipolar disorder, borderline personality disorder, etc.).

In my own experience, no amount of mental health resources would have been enough to address my symptoms of schizophrenia without a proper diagnosis of mental illness, medication, and treatment. Even though I didn't learn about schizophrenia or mental illness much in high school, I was fairly well educated in both mental health and mental illness because of my time spent as a caregiver for my mother with schizoaffective disorder. Despite the knowledge I gained as a caregiver, my own experiences with psychosis made it difficult for me to understand that I was in need of help. So, I never reached out for help. Of course, with an illness like schizophrenia, it may become obvious to others in your life that you may be experiencing some sort of crisis. People in my life started offering me general mental health support, but without the insight that medication and treatment provided, it would take me years to properly address my illness.

When I was first able to reach out for help, I did not think that I had schizophrenia. I was unable to see the symptoms in myself. I just started to notice that I wasn't able to do what everyone around me could do. I couldn't hold a job. I had to drop out of college. I felt that I needed my addictions just to get through each day. I was always confused about my surroundings and the situations I found myself in, and I was constantly depressed, anxious, and scared. So, I decided to see if there was something wrong with me.

Little did I know that my wife and mom had been preparing resources in hopes that I would have enough clarity to reach out for help. They got me into a doctor that was able to evaluate me and refer me to a psychiatrist who diagnosed me with undifferentiated schizophrenia. Schizophrenia is an illness that causes hallucinations, delusions, and paranoia and can affect a person's ability to think, feel, and behave clearly. Schizophrenia affects roughly 1% of the US population. Even after getting the diagnosis, it would take months of being on antipsychotic medication before I would be able to come to terms with my diagnosis or the idea that I would have a lifelong mental illness.

After I came to terms with my diagnosis, I started learning more about mental illness and my diagnosis specifically. Schizophrenia has three types of symptom domains: positive symptoms, negative symptoms, and cognitive symptoms. Being more educated about my schizophrenia diagnosis made it easier to find coping mechanisms and ways to be more involved in my own care. Learning about these symptom domains would help me better understand how my illness could affect every aspect of my life. This is what I learned about these symptom domains:

- **Positive symptoms:** These are the symptoms of schizophrenia that most people are aware of like hallucinations, delusions, and paranoia. There is often a confusion that "positive" symptoms are "good." Positive just means "in addition to," as these symptoms are an addition to the individual's personality, whereas negative symptoms are a deficit and take away from an individual's personality.

- **Negative symptoms:** These symptoms greatly affect a patient's quality of life and functioning. These symptoms consist of social isolation/withdrawal, inability to express emotions, difficulties with communication, and lack of motivation. I did not learn about these symptoms until later in my diagnosis and thought that all of these issues were a fault of my own.

- **Cognitive symptoms:** This symptom domain involves a person's ability to think and remember. These symptoms include lack of energy, issues with memory, and deficits in learning and retention.

Once I did finally receive a proper diagnosis and learned more about it, after several years of self-medicating through addiction and being incarcerated, I thought that my medications would cure everything. I thought I would never have to worry about symptoms of my schizophrenia and definitely not any other mental health issues. Unfortunately, I think doctors and care providers could do better at communicating that the ongoing need for care, managing/adjusting medications, monitoring symptoms, and focusing on self-care will be lifelong considerations.

Why Early Intervention Is Important

Mental illness and mental health, while different, are linked. In fact, there are many correlations between the two, and it is possible to have both. Most of my mental health issues like anxiety, depression, and suicidal ideology came *after* I was on medication for schizophrenia and stable, starting to live a "normal" life again. My entire adult life was spent learning to live with and manage my schizophrenia diagnosis and the accompanying ongoing mental health issues. I went on to experience major depressive episodes and issues with anxiety that made it incredibly difficult to keep a job when I finally started working again.

I am happy to be seeing that general mental health resources (both in the workplace and in clinical settings) are starting to ensure that those who need additional help outside of talk therapy or counseling are able to get the proper referrals and specialists to help individuals get early intervention.

> Early intervention is the most effective way to help people struggling with undiagnosed mental illnesses get the help they need before symptoms start affecting every aspect of that person's life or begin causing long-term cognitive damage.

The result of people *not* getting early intervention to mental illness can have lifelong consequences. Untreated mental illness leads to unreversible cognitive damage, severe behavioral problems, and physical health issues. Not getting treatment can also lead to issues with addiction, incarceration, and homelessness. People with mental illness make up some of the highest rates of these different issues. For example, people with schizophrenia make up less than 1% of the population but are estimated to make up over 20% of the homelessness population.[2] Also,

---

[2]https://www.nami.org/about-mental-illness/mental-health-by-the-numbers/#mental-illness-and-the-criminal-justice-system

a third of adults with mental illness struggle with substance abuse disorder (SAD), more than twice the rate for those with no psychiatric disorder.[3] These are just some of the examples of how a mental illness diagnosis can forever alter a person's life.

The main focus of this book will be to talk about the importance of all mental health in the workplace, including my personal stories of working with both symptoms of schizophrenia and the resulting effects of negative mental health. I also feature the stories of two friends and mental health advocates, Gabe Howard and Michelle Hamme – who both struggle with mental health issues and diagnosed mental illnesses – to show how their employers could have done more to help them thrive at work by being more understanding and by providing additional accommodations and resources.

So, although mental health is the main focus of conversation, it is important to understand mental illness and how it can affect individuals and also acknowledge the need for more education and understanding for *both* in the workplace – especially when having conversations with management or coworkers who may not understand what mental health really is. When I started working, I quickly realized that many people were not educated about mental health or mental illness, and they could even be cruel about it.

---

[3] https://www.nami.org/about-mental-illness/mental-health-by-the-numbers

Chapter 3

Stigma at the Watercooler
Addressing Misconceptions about Mental Health at Work

"I don't think I can work with Beth now, knowing that she's crazy. She was even in the psych ward and is on medications now," said a coworker rather loudly.

"Do you think it will be safe to work with her? What if she freaks out while she's here?" another office worker responded.

This was a real conversation I overheard between two coworkers while working as a custodian at an office job. They were talking about another coworker who had spent a few days in psychiatric care with depression and suicidal ideology after some life changes. She was expected back the following week.

Little did they know they were having this conversation less than 10 feet from someone who had just had a brief psychiatric stay as well. I couldn't believe they were just having this conversation so casually in the open breakroom, not whispering, not even considering how incredibly insensitive they were being.

I was shocked that they would speak so poorly about a coworker who worked in the same department as they. In fact, I had seen both these coworkers interact with Beth constantly. They probably saw her outside of work or even had drinks with her after work sometimes! Beth was always very kind, and prior to this breakroom interaction, I had never heard anyone speak poorly about her before. However, just because Beth experienced some mental health issues, they said things like this:

- "There's no way she is going to be able to keep up with the work now."
- "She should find an easier job if she can't handle this one."
- "She's probably just faking it to get some time away from work. Maybe I should do that too."

And they both laughed as the made their way back from the breakroom to their cubicles.

It was so hard to hear them say these things about our coworker because at this point in my life I had also been in crisis that required time away from work. I had heard these types of statements said to me or about me too. It was so hurtful, and the things they were saying were incredibly frustrating.

We're Not Making It Up

The idea that a person would fake a struggle with mental health always baffled me. I couldn't believe that this was even a real conversation between adults. To think someone would want to mock others at work and in a small community – it didn't just stay at work; it would eventually become a conversation in the town too. To endure the gossip, but also the embarrassment of coming back to face these people, and to take on the bills involved with a hospital stay – why would someone want that?

The idea that people with chronic or invisible illnesses all must be faking simply because we don't "look" disabled is an unfortunate myth that people with certain illnesses or diagnoses face each day. It only furthers the point that many people don't understand certain conditions. Mental health constantly gets ridiculed largely because it is not obvious or as visible as a physical injury or illness. As I continue to advocate, my goal is that eventually more people will treat mental health and mental illness with the same urgency and thoroughness with which people approach physical care. If your coworker had a broken arm, you wouldn't accuse them of faking, would you?

I wish I could say that was the first or last time I overheard a coworker mocking someone for mental health struggles in the workplace. Having worked in many different industries, I have seen people mock and discriminate against myself and other coworkers with mental health issues or mental illness just for needing to use accommodations, FMLA, or other company-provided mental health resources (something we'll talk more about in Chapter 5). I wish I could say this was exclusive to one industry or type of business, but unfortunately these conversations happen in almost every workplace I've been in. I don't believe that people do this because they intend to be inconsiderate or rude but because they don't have enough knowledge or education about mental health.

I had another experience while I was working in a manufacturing job, and I heard a shift manager belittle a coworker of ours for calling in for a "mental health day." To be clear, this person decided to use their accrued personal time off (PTO) because they were dealing with severe anxiety. Every person on my shift had something negative to say about this, including the manager who told everyone that was why they called in.

"Can you believe that? A mental health day? What do they think this is, a cushy desk job?" said the shift manager to a coworker of mine as they both began to laugh about the idea that he could be anxious enough to call in.

At this point in my career, I had not opened up yet about my diagnosis or my mental health struggles and had not started advocating for myself, or others, in the workplace yet. I felt like what the coworker did was very reasonable. Looking back, I regret not speaking up for my coworker. It would have been a great time to try to educate my coworkers about mental health, burnout, and self-care. I didn't understand why all of my coworkers were so upset and irritated about the idea of needing a "mental health day" because I don't think any of them would have been upset had the coworker called in sick or with a physical ailment.

I remember an older coworker saying, "This new generation will do anything to get out of work, even make up fake conditions just to not have to come in. Everyone has anxiety, ADHD, or autism now, and none of them want to work anymore."

I didn't even know what to say to him, so I said nothing because I didn't want to be confrontational. But as someone who has been around mental illness and struggled with my own diagnosis for my entire adult life, I was so confused how he could think that people were faking well-documented and studied illnesses and disorders. In my experience with my own mental health and having been a caregiver as well, I knew that people didn't fake having mental health issues; people faked being okay.

We're Allowed to Take Care of Ourselves

Before my official diagnosis, I remember telling a manager at a production job in a factory that I was feeling incredibly anxious and would not be able to make it into work that day, and he actually responded, "What are you, a child? If you are not throwing up or sick, then you need to be here."

And because I wanted to prove so bad that I was a "team player" or a good worker, I still came in. I should have trusted my body and my brain because I had to leave that night after fainting due to my symptoms becoming so severe. This led to me getting a writeup for an unexcused absence. It was instances like this that made me realize how little my peers understood mental health and how little certain employers cared about me and my struggles with mental health.

I remember the first time I had to leave work with symptoms of mental health issues. When I came back to work, I remember certain people not talking to me anymore and other people making backhanded comments like "I hope you enjoyed your day off" or "Wish I could've left too, too bad I got bills to pay." These were people that I considered friends. They were people that I thought cared about me and my well-being, but none of them asked if I was okay or even why I left. My closest work acquaintance told me that while I was away, people found out I left because I was feeling anxious and depressed and that it had become an ongoing joke between coworkers.

I was devastated hearing this, especially because I didn't want to leave. I wanted to be at work; I had bills to pay and was planning a wedding. It didn't make any sense to me why they would mock me or say these things about me, so I started working myself to burnout just trying to maintain this image that I was doing fine or that I could do what everyone else did, but I could only maintain that charade for so long, and it always had such a negative impact on both my mental and physical health.

Every job that I worked, I would have people talk about me for either taking time off due to my mental health or how I couldn't keep up some days and should find another job. Because I would have negative and cognitive symptoms, people would treat me poorly for having issues with memory or performance. This made me want to leave work or call in, but I knew they would judge me for that too. It was a no-win scenario for me.

I wish I could say this was just coworker gossip, but I even heard these comments from managers and leads. This is probably why 74% of full-time employees in the United States say it is appropriate to discuss mental health concerns at work, but only 58% say they feel comfortable sharing about their mental health at work (2024 NAMI Workplace Poll).[1]

These unfortunate scenarios also led to people I worked with constantly talking about me both in front of me and behind my back. That would forever change my ability to communicate effectively about my concerns regarding the workplace and also about my own limitations and my needed accommodations. For several years I was unable to advocate for myself or set boundaries, and that would eventually lead to burnout, and I would get fired and have to leave several jobs all because I was afraid how people I worked with would react or what they would say about me.

Other Misconceptions

In this same job I would go on to hear more misconceptions about mental health and mental illness than in any other job or industry that I would ever work in. People would make claims like

- "People with mental health issues are just weak, they choose to be negative."

---

[1] https://www.nami.org/support-education/publications-reports/survey-reports/the-2024-nami-workplace-mental-health-poll

- "Mental illnesses and mental health issues aren't real; they are just excuses that people use to not have to work and get disability."

- "Mental health issues are a result of poor parenting and not disciplining kids enough. Kids are just too spoiled now, and that's why they grow up with these issues."

- "Only drug addicts have mental health issues or diagnoses like schizophrenia."

- "People with schizophrenia and other mental illnesses should just be locked up because they are useless to society and dangerous."

My coworkers would say these things to my face, not knowing that I had a mother with schizophrenia or that I myself was in the process of receiving a schizophrenia diagnosis. I knew that some of these misconceptions existed, but I didn't know they were so common in my own community, let alone thought by people I worked with every day. It was so hard to feel comfortable at this job knowing how everyone had these incorrect and harmful ideas about individuals like me.

There are so many misconceptions out there about mental health and mental illness. People think that having struggles with mental health makes you less reliable, more dangerous, less trustworthy, or even less employable. I have been told that I am "more dangerous" simply for having a schizophrenia diagnosis despite never causing intentional harm to anyone in my entire life. Just a diagnosis or acting differently can change how people look at you. Words like *depression*, *OCD*, and *anxiety* have even been so misused in casual conversation that they are often diminished to less serious than what they really are. They are so misused that many people can't even tell you what obsessive-compulsive disorder and other diagnoses actually entail.

Saying things like "I am so OCD because I need my desk to be cleaned off" or "the weather is so bipolar today" not only increases the stigma of the words but also shows that people often don't understand the symptoms and diagnosis that can be devastating to some people's lives. People say things like this constantly in the workplace with no regard to who may be hearing it or what the people around them might have been through. I even had a coworker tell me that depression and anxiety were fake and that people used these symptoms as an excuse.

He claimed that people needed to just get over it because "everyone gets sad sometimes." He said this to me in my early stages of my symptoms, in the height of my struggles with anxiety and depression, and hearing this made me believe him, which kept me from reaching out for help sooner. I figured if he was right, then I just needed to toughen up and get through it.

This once again shows how people who are not educated about mental health can say something that can detrimentally affect another person's view of themselves or someone they know who may be experiencing negative mental health.

We Are Allowed to Speak Up

Before I could ever get to a point where I would be able to discuss my mental health with a manager or with human resources, I started trying to find ways to address these conversations whenever I heard them. Whether I heard negative gossip about me or another coworker, I felt like I needed to start shutting it down. This is something I wouldn't have been able to do without attending peer support groups and learning more about mental health and mental illness from the perspective of other people living with it.

Educating myself and talking to peers with mental health issues allowed me to interject when I heard people sharing common misconceptions in the workplace. I could confidently inform my coworkers and sometimes even managers who made remarks about anyone who may have been dealing with mental health concerns. Although this may not have made the biggest difference, and certainly did not change how workplaces across the world spoke about mental health, it started the right positive conversations in my own environment. I felt that even the smallest changes were monuments if the workplace was extremely toxic. People would stop making those comments and jokes around me. These were small wins, but it was my introduction to being able to set boundaries and advocate for myself and others.

The reason correcting misconceptions is so important is because it is another form of mental health awareness. It provides someone with more information about a topic that they may be misinformed about; as I said earlier, I have come to find through advocacy that most negative comments about mental health come from a lack of education and ignorance of the topic.

The more time I spent around people sharing misinformation, the more I realized they just didn't have the facts about the issues they were discussing and had likely never been around someone with lived experience. Mental health and mental illness are difficult to discuss not just in the workplace but anywhere. That is the problem. Even online, I see so many uninformed and ignorant comments. Most of the people I know (especially in my small hometown) were told by parents or grandparents that mental illness wasn't real or that mental health issues were just for weak people.

Knowing that I was not combating real anger toward people with mental health issues but ignorance and a lack of knowledge on the issues on the topic made me feel much more able to start conversations and speak up when I knew I could provide more insight. This was never confrontational but was just making sure that they had additional data and information while they considered a situation with a coworker who may have FMLA for mental illness or someone needing to leave early due to an unforeseen mental health issue. Many people don't understand how common mental health issues are. Some people I spoke to didn't even realize that some symptoms (including physical symptoms) that they themselves had had in the past could be due to declining mental health.

I also noticed a change in perspective, attitudes, and outlooks in the workplaces where I openly discussed my personal experiences with mental health and as a caregiver for someone with mental illness. While working in a manufacturing facility, I saw more of my coworkers come to me in confidence and ask follow-up questions about some of the topics or statistics that I discussed.

I made a very close friend at this job because when he heard my stories, he was able to relate as a caregiver for someone in his family with mental illness. He told me how he was always too afraid to talk about his own issues because of how our peers made jokes about the same conditions that he and his loved one struggled with. I explained that that was why I tended to probably overshare: because I came from incredibly toxic workplaces where I never spoke up at and felt so isolated.

I would have many encounters like this over the years of realizing that I was not alone. I was not alone as someone with mental health issues. I was not alone as someone with a diagnosed mental illness. I was not alone as a caregiver. Everyone can feel like they are alone in their journey or like no one can understand what they are going through, but realizing that others have had similar experiences made me feel so seen and understood. That is why it is so important to speak up, share our stories, and keep people from spreading harmful stereotypes and misconceptions about mental health.

Part II

Being on the Job with Mental Health Issues

Chapter 4

"Should I Tell My Boss?"
Starting the Conversation

I don't want to make it seem like starting conversations with your employer is always easy or isn't frightening. I would be lying if I didn't admit that I know some mental health advocates who were fired shortly after disclosing their illness or mental health concerns. As I explained in Chapter 1, I was terrified to have the conversation with my HR manager. It is hard enough to admit that you are struggling with mental health, and saying it out loud to your boss can be an incredibly intimidating experience. I remember feeling incredibly alone and like I was failing myself and my family for not being able to function like everyone else.

But the conversation is worth it. It was so exhausting having to worry about whether I was going to lose my job for having symptoms or having people find out about my diagnosis or trying to mask to the point of burnout. Not telling company leadership about my mental health issues seemed like an easier choice at the time, but once I finally became comfortable having that conversation, it made work so much easier for me. I realize in hindsight I spent so much time and energy hiding my struggles, when addressing it up front made my day-to-day work life much more possible.

I was able to ask for accommodations and not have to try to "mask" every single day I came to work. I found resources like the FMLA, which allowed me to take necessary time off without the fear of losing my job. Having this critical conversation with HR and my manager took a load off my mind and, in doing so, actually improved my mental health. Making the decision to have the conversation was the hardest part, but I have never looked back.

Deciding to Tell Your Boss

I now know that making mental health conversations more common allows employers and managers to better understand the needs of their workers *before* an employee has to approach them about any concerns they may have. Addressing mental health at work also allows employees to feel more comfortable in talking about issues if they realize that they are not alone and that it is okay to not feel okay.

Okay, but When Is the Best Time to Bring It Up?

I always get questions about when it is appropriate to start talking about mental health concerns with your employer. Do you wait until you are in crisis? Do you tell them in your job interview? Or do you tell them when they start writing you up for performance and attendance issues related to your mental health?

It took many years of mental health struggles in many different jobs for me to understand the most effective ways to address my mental health and to be certain that my employer was equipped to help me effectively. I personally found it most effective to talk with HR about my diagnosis and any ongoing mental health issues immediately *after* being offered the job.

So no, I do not bring up my diagnosis or mental health issues in the job interview process. You are not legally required to disclose any sort of medical conditions (including mental health conditions) in a job interview *even if asked*.

I once had a situation where I was asked about my health conditions when I was being interviewed for a job, and I simply refused to disclose and asked to move on. The Americans with Disabilities Act (ADA) bars employers from asking questions about any disabilities or mental conditions during an interview. I ended up getting the job and disclosing to HR after I had been officially hired.

> The ADA bars employers from asking questions about a candidate's mental condition during a job interview.

Oftentimes people don't want to seem confrontational in an interview and, when asked, just answer the question to make the interview go smoother. I later found out that the reason my interviewer didn't know not to ask that question was because he was a manager but not trained in HR.

In my own experience, the few times I did try to disclose my concerns beforehand, I would not receive a call back or a job offer. Although it is illegal for companies to discriminate against people with disabilities, it still happens. I don't want there to be any chance that me having ongoing mental health issues will be the reason I don't get a job. If a company is comparing my résumé with an identical résumé, my mental health issues should not be a determining factor. So, I stopped disclosing my condition during the interview process (which, again, is my right by law).

I admit that having mental health issues and working at certain jobs does require a good fit. So, during the interview process, if I want to learn more about a company's mental health accessibility, I have the most success finding accommodating workplaces by asking a question at the end of the interview like these:

- "Does your company work with an Employee Assistance Program or any other employee wellness resources?"

- "Can you tell me more about your company culture?"

- "Wellness is a topic that is important to me and my family. Does your company do anything to promote safety, personal well-being, or mental health awareness?"

The answers to these questions, although indirect from asking "how would your company react to me having a mental health crisis?," will display an employer's willingness to even discuss mental health in an interview. Any job recruiter would agree that it is important to ask questions at the end of an interview to show your interest and engagement, so this would be an option in addition to more specific job-related questions. Asking an interview question like this can lead to good conversations about how the company addresses topics like mental health and employee well-being.

> You can also do a little proactive research on the company's website before the interview to see if they offer any wellness programs for employees. Then you can ask even more company-specific questions like "I see your company offers a wellness benefit to employees. What sorts of things can that be used for?"

If I get through the interview process and am successful with getting a job offer, I still wait for the hiring process to be completed, and that is when I recommend having a conversation with HR about any diagnosis or ongoing mental health issues. I found that it can be really effective to have the conversation early instead of trying to address it only after receiving reprimands for declining performance or an attendance issue.

By informing HR, you can set a precedent that although you can do this job and meet its goals, you may eventually need to work with HR to find resources or accommodations if you have mental health issues that you have struggled with in the past. Having conversations with management or coworkers after that is up to you, and such conversations can have both positive and negative results depending on the type of job and industry. Having that initial conversation with HR can pave the way for effective communication while employed.

Should You Trust HR?

I know that some people don't trust HR and sometimes even dislike them. There is an idea in many workplaces – especially nonoffice jobs like manufacturing, distribution, etc. – that human resources employees care only about the company and can't help employees with problems they are dealing with. In many of these industries, I would hear my coworkers say that HR was not to be trusted and that they were looking for any reason to fire you. That is not the reason companies have human resources departments and not the reason people pursue HR careers.

In my experience from pursuing an HR degree and meeting many emerging HR professionals, they often pursue the career with an intention to retain employees and help them thrive within a company. In fact, HR professionals are often the very reason that many companies now offer mental health services and resources.

Now, there will always be companies or individuals who will not act in the best interest of the employees or individuals, but my hope is that as workers start to have these discussions and set boundaries, employers will adapt to a more mental health–friendly culture. A company having an

HR team can usually be a more accommodating workplace because they will know the rights and laws protecting workers with disabilities, whereas a small company without HR may not know these rules – or may choose to ignore them. I have already seen some of this change occurring in my own workplace experiences over the last few years. Assuming that all managers or HR managers are the enemy prevents many people from reaching out for help at work and may keep them from knowing about very important resources that the company may offer.

Part of the reason that managers and HR professionals can be underutilized is that in some of the industries I have worked in and spoken to, there are negative ideas about leadership that tend to start with employees. This could be a result of a negative work environment or just an individual or small group of employees that feel like managers or HR don't have the employees' best interest in mind.

I saw this more often in nonoffice type roles; it was usually worse in production and manufacturing facilities. I once started a new job in which on my first day the trainer told me that I should not go to my shift manager or HR about anything because they only had the company's interest in mind. Again, this was not a random worker but the person who was chosen by the managers to individually onboard employees. This made me question the employee, the leadership, and company culture.

If you hear about an employee who may be encouraging coworkers to not reach out with questions, it needs to be addressed immediately. That can create a poor company image and a toxic work environment, especially if that person is working closely or training new hires as this person was in my case.

If You're Still Not Convinced

Many people have told me that they waited to tell their employers about their mental health conditions until they didn't have a choice or the issues became severe enough that they couldn't hide them anymore. There are many possible outcomes to being open and honest with your employer. I will share three of my own experiences about reaching out to management and HR regarding my mental health issues:

- The first is when I told my manager after having some issues on the job and it went poorly.
- The second is about not telling anyone until it led to burnout and I was fired by my employer.
- The last is when I reached out to HR early and the situation was handled perfectly.

Telling the Wrong Person

While writing this book about overcoming mental health conversations at work, I wish that I only had positive stories to tell. Unfortunately, as far as we have come as a workforce in addressing mental health awareness, there are still many employers who still have a long way to go in understanding the needs of their employees and providing the right resources and accommodations for those needs. The first story about my negative experiences in the workplace shows this and how my management team could have assisted me more and retained an employee in the process.

While working in production, I worked for several years in a factory for a company with fewer than 100 employees. There was only one person in the HR department, and the shift managers reported directly to them. While at this job I had a series of mental health issues, and it led to me missing a few days of work. Instead of going to HR, I went to my direct manager, which I now know was a mistake. You will want to include HR immediately to act as a mediator and to also document conversations so that you can address any concerning or inappropriate actions that management may take against you.

When telling my direct manager that I was feeling depressed and was struggling to get through the workday, he jokingly said, "That must be the reason why your production numbers are down," and then told me to just "leave my issues at the door" and I would get through it. That was the entire conversation, and then he walked away.

I still think about this conversation because I genuinely don't think he was trying to be mean or inconsiderate. It seemed like he was just too uncomfortable with the topic to take it seriously. I overall enjoyed working with this manager, but after I had this conversation, I noticed that he spoke to me less, trusted my judgment less, and stopped telling me about new opportunities with the company. It is important to remember that most managers or supervisors are not trained in HR matters. And a lot of people are still not comfortable talking about issues like mental health in general. So if you talk to someone in HR, you are at least more likely to find someone who has been trained in HR topics like legal accommodations for mental health conditions, disabled workers rights, and more.

> Remember, most managers are not trained in HR matters. And a lot of people are just not comfortable talking about mental health in general. Unfortunately, we're just not there as a society yet. So if you talk to someone in HR, you are at least more likely to find someone who has been trained in HR topics like legal accommodations for mental health conditions and more.

This was one of my first jobs after my issues with addiction and incarceration, so I felt like I had to be loyal despite feeling like the company and management didn't care about me as an individual. I eventually realized that the management and company didn't care about my general safety, let alone my mental health. I had to quit abruptly when my paid time off ran out and I had received several writeups. Knowing what I know now, I would have brought my mental health concerns and my reasonable accommodation needs to HR instead of trying to confide in my direct manager.

Telling Too Late

I had been working as a server in a restaurant for several years, both as my primary job and for a while as a second job. There are many factors of working in the service industry that can lead to additional stress, including a constantly fast-paced environment, rude and insulting customers, and financial instability. It is enough to send anyone over the edge.

All these stress factors contributed negatively to my mental health, and while working as a server I would get such severe anxiety that I would get episodes of catatonia where I would be unable to move, like I was frozen. On certain days, I actually really enjoyed this job, which is why I kept it so long. Unfortunately, it was such a small restaurant that there was no direct manager or HR department I could go to with concerns, just the owner of the business.

I was too nervous to reach out, and the owner did actually check on me throughout my time there to see if I was all right whenever he would notice that my work performance was declining. As I will talk about in Chapter 6, the issue with "masking" or pretending to be fine all the time is that you can only do it for so long before it becomes noticeable or it leads to burnout.

Whenever he would ask me about my declining performance or sudden inability to do the job, I would just tell him, "I am fine." After a while, I could tell he was frustrated because I had inconsistency with my performance, and

I never explained to him that I was dealing with mental health issues.

In my last few months there, I started to really decline, and I couldn't mask my symptoms anymore. I was dealing with a depressive episode that caused me to have less patience with guests and made self-care and personal hygiene nearly impossible. I couldn't fake being okay anymore, and trying to mask led me to complete burnout.

It got worse and worse because I also was being put on the schedule less and less, which caused financial stress and increased my anxiety too. It got to a point where I was only on the schedule once a week, and when I asked for more hours, the owner told me about his concerns with my attitude, performance, and hygiene and explained that he would not be giving me any more hours and would actually be cutting them completely.

I was so angry about being fired at the time after working there for five years. Suddenly I had to find a new job while dealing with all these issues. I look back with frustration on this particular employment experience because years later I returned to work for the same boss after I had my diagnosis and was more stable, and he was great to work for and very understanding.

This is a great example of how communicating my mental health concerns helped someone understand why these problems were constantly recurring. It is also a great example of how masking may allow someone to skate by for a long time but can ultimately lead to severe burnout.

The Ideal Situation

The third and final story about telling my employer about my mental health issues was my last job before pursuing advocacy and motivational speaking full-time. This job was in customer service and sales, so it was more of an office role than my previous workforce experience. This was my best experience with an employer not just acknowledging my mental health but also supporting me without question.

At this point in my journey, I had been through lots of experiences with working in different types of industries, addressing mental health in the workplace, setting boundaries, using workplace resources, and talking to leadership about my schizophrenia diagnosis and general mental health accommodations. All those experiences varied depending on when I had those conversations and on the companies that I worked for at the time.

I knew based on my previous employment experiences that it was best to address my diagnosis and mental health needs immediately after receiving a job offer and signing the paperwork. I also knew to start by having that conversation with human resources instead of a manager or a coworker.

After HR knew what to expect, I waited until I felt comfortable and spoke to my hiring manager after I had been working with them for a few weeks, and I even had open conversations about schizophrenia and mental health with all of my coworkers. Telling my coworkers about my diagnosis was something I always avoided and was nervous to do in this role. This allowed coworkers to ask me questions about my mental health when they noticed me struggling, which gave me so many more people I could talk to about any concern that came up with anxiety, depression, medication changes, or symptoms of my mental illness.

My manager not only acknowledged my mental illness and made efforts to constantly check in on me, but he also celebrated my accomplishments as I started to do more with social media, advocacy, and mental health awareness, and so did my coworkers. It was so freeing to not have to constantly mask my symptoms and emotions.

People often agree with my premise of *why* they should talk to the HR manager and usually follow up with "But *when* is a good time to start a conversation with my boss?" My response is always that starting a conversation is less about timing and more about assessing the HR professional, company, and culture. If you are working somewhere that has a negative workplace culture or toxic employees, then it won't matter when you have the conversation because it is unlikely that a negative workplace will be willing to work collaboratively to make it more accommodating. This is also true in reverse; if it is a positive company culture, it won't matter because it shouldn't be an issue for any employer to accommodate and provide resources for you.

Having an open dialogue and honest conversation with a new employer is something that you should do as soon as possible. The sooner that these conversations happen, the sooner you can have relief knowing that if you have a mental health crisis or ongoing struggle, they already have a background and awareness of your situation, which prevents needing to address such a sensitive topic while in crisis. Having the conversation with your manager can also prompt a conversation about the resources and accommodations you need and are entitled to by law, something we'll discuss in the next chapter.

Chapter 5

Understanding Accommodations and Your Rights

Once you've had the conversations with leadership about your mental health concerns or your diagnosed mental illness, you should follow up by requesting information regarding any resources your employer may have. This could include an EAP, FMLA, short-term disability, or other reasonable accommodations. Some of these resources may require follow-up information or an official diagnosis, but there are resources you can request with almost no up-front information. In this chapter, I will share my personal experience with some of these resources – how I found them, how I used them, and how they helped me be more productive, comfortable, and happy in my jobs.

Employees who struggle may need a variety of things to feel safe and secure. This can include programs, peer support, education, accommodations, mental health resources, and even just access to healthcare and insurance. In fact, 9 in 10 employees say employer-sponsored mental healthcare coverage is important for creating a positive workplace culture.[1] This is true for employees regardless of gender, age, stage in career, or managerial status.

---

[1] https://www.nami.org/Support-Education/Publications-Reports/Survey-Reports/The-2024-NAMI-Workplace-Mental-Health-Poll

Employee Assistance Programs

I have personally utilized almost all of the resources that most employers provide. The very first resource that I was told to utilize was the EAP. Generally, an employee assistance program is a 1-800 number that is available 24/7 that provides free and confidential assessments, short-term counseling, referrals, and follow-up services to employees (and sometimes their families) who have personal or work-related problems such as stress management, family or marital issues, health and mental health issues, addictions and compulsive behavior, and more. As I continue to travel and speak at different companies, I am pleased to find that most major companies in the United States have an EAP that employees can call for counseling and other resources. I have used an EAP at several companies with similar experiences.

The first time I called an EAP was when I was 18 years old while working in a retail position in college. I was a year into the job, and I had just received a promotion and was finding myself depressed, stressed, and anxious. I had not yet started having symptoms of schizophrenia. I was just finding myself in burnout from trying to maintain a full-time overnight job, being on my own for the first time, and being a full-time student. It was an unfortunate stressor of growing up in poverty that in order to afford school, I needed to work at the same time.

At this point in my life, I had never talked to anyone about any sort of mental health issues – not a therapist, my significant other, or my friends, not even my mother. I told my manager that I was struggling to keep up with work and my personal life. The manager basically told me that I would have to just "figure it out" or find a new job. I was deciding whether I would have to quit when I confided in a coworker about the conversation, and I was lucky that the person was someone who also had mental health issues and was familiar with the company's EAP.

He told me about the program and gave me the number to call. I had never heard of an EAP, and I had no idea what it was or what services it provided. I am amazed that it took another employee to give me the resources that management or the HR team should've provided. I can't be sure whether this was negligence on the part of my shift manager or he was never trained to know and refer these resources.

I had the number, but it took me a week or two to get enough courage to make the first call. I remember the call well because I felt ashamed even making it. I felt like I was weak because other people were able to balance work and their personal lives. When I finally made the call, I was met with a very caring and empathetic voice. She didn't ask anything more than what she needed in order to refer me to a local counseling service. I was so afraid of calling, so I was so glad that it was an easy and quick process. The EAP allowed me to have six free counseling appointments, which I would not have been able to afford otherwise. My needs would eventually require more than just counseling or talk therapy, but at that time it was perfect. I was able to talk through some of my stresses, anxieties, and other issues that were causing me to fall into burnout.

These counseling sessions allowed me to work through enough of my mental health issues to get me stable enough to be productive and happy at work again. I even got a referral to a psychiatrist, which I decided not to utilize because at the time, I didn't think I needed it, and I was also afraid of the stigma around medication and treatment, so I only did the bare minimum to feel good enough to get through each day. Overall, my first experience using an EAP was effective; however, after my schizophrenia symptoms began, my future EAP experiences were less successful.

I was unable to get or hold a job for very long after my mental illness symptoms began because I was in such a delusional mindset and was having severe symptoms like hallucinations and paranoid thoughts. However, I was delusional enough that I didn't believe anything was wrong with me. As I said previously, I would spend the next several years undiagnosed and struggling with addiction and incarceration; it wasn't until I got out of jail that I was able to hold a job long enough to be able to start accessing resources again. That job would also be my next experience with an EAP.

I remembered how I was able to speak to a counselor at my previous job and how it had given me some stability. So, I asked the manager at this new job about the EAP, and he had no idea what I was talking about. I thought that maybe this company just did not have an EAP. However, when I spoke to human resources the next morning, the HR manager said that they did have an EAP and that all of the managers should have been aware of this. This is why it can be so important to involve HR in the conversation. Sometimes managers do not have all of the information they should have.

I had just left a restaurant/serving job before starting this manufacturing job in a factory. I had dealt with a lot of negative people (coworkers) and situations in this work environment, with very little assistance from leadership, but they did at least have an EAP. This time when getting referred to a counselor, I didn't know what was wrong with me, but I knew I needed more help from a specialist. Unfortunately, the counselor I met with had no interest in referring me to a specialist. I ended up getting so irritated that I used only two of the appointments and stopped going.

At this time, I was hiding my symptoms from everyone and hadn't even told my own family what I was dealing with. Reaching out to an EAP and not getting help was disappointing and a huge setback at the time. I am lucky I had friends and family to turn to. I have heard of others having experiences like this, where people with mental illness or more serious mental health issues feel lost or alone after the free sessions provided by an EAP.

However, I have heard of other people who have had success getting referrals and follow-ups after the initial EAP appointments. And, after I got stable on my medication and treatment, I have used an EAP at almost every employer I have had and found that those free therapy appointments were so important in different times in my life while struggling with situational mental health struggles. Overall, I do recommend EAPs as a good resource, especially for those looking for referrals, people who don't have a therapist or someone to talk to, and people just starting to address their own mental health struggles.

Family Medical Leave Act

Employees can also seek time-based accommodations for mental health support. In fact, nearly half (48%) of US employees believe that paid or unpaid time off is the most valuable accommodation for their mental health, followed by flexible schedules, which could include part-time hours, job sharing, or adjustments to their starting and ending times, according to SHRM Research.[2]

In my own journey, the Family Medical Leave Act (FMLA) of 1993 may be the most crucial resource I ever had. In the experience I related in Chapter 1, the very first resource that my HR manager told me about was FMLA and how I may be able to use it to ensure that I didn't lose my job just for having schizophrenia symptoms or for having mental health struggles.

FMLA allows employees of covered employers to take unpaid time off for either family or personal medical

---

[2] https://www.shrm.org/content/dam/en/shrm/executive-network/en-insights-forums/May%202023%20EN%20Insights%20Forum%20Recap%20-%20Mental%20Health%20in%20the%20Workplace%20(2).pdf

reasons. It allows eligible employees to take unpaid, job-protected leave for serious health conditions, including mental health issues. State laws may offer additional protections and benefits, so it is important to familiarize yourself with the specific regulations in your area. For instance, in the state I live in, Wisconsin, the state only allows 10 weeks of unpaid time each year, whereas the federal FMLA allows for 12 weeks. Wisconsin also requires 1000 hours worked before becoming eligible to apply, whereas other states may require as few as 0 hours. These are just a few of the examples of how FMLA may differ from state to state.

FMLA can be used for many different occurrences like births, serious injury, and even adoption. Although getting approved for FMLA was a longer process than some other resources, it really protected me from losing my job for taking time off during my recovery journey.

There are a few stipulations to FMLA, which can make it more difficult to get approved for than other things. It does require you to be employed with the same employer for at least a year. This can be very difficult for those who are really struggling with their mental health and is a notable hurdle for many. A few other limitations to the Family Medical Leave Act are that it is unpaid time off and is capped at 12 weeks. I was fortunate enough to have a spouse who was able to help me financially as I used this unpaid time, but I also want to acknowledge that I understand not everyone will be able to afford to do this, in which case other resources may need to be explored.

If you do qualify because you've worked at a job for a year, you can speak with both your employer and your healthcare provider to discuss applying for FMLA. I have heard from other advocates and patients that it can sometimes be difficult to get approved for FMLA without a formal diagnosis. This is where a referral may be needed to a specialist, and it may be effective to use an employee assistance program to get a referral to a psychiatrist or psychologist for diagnosis if it is warranted for the individual. Human resources and your care team can help you through the process of applying, and if you get approved, every company has different rules for using your approved time.

I had FMLA at my last three jobs, and it allowed me to take time off without having to explain my symptoms or issues with my managers. I could use the time unpaid as needed just to make sure that I didn't lose my job for having mental health issues or a mental illness diagnosis. You will have to work closely with HR and have open communication in order to use FMLA correctly. Different companies will have different ways of implementing unpaid time off, and some will even use third-party companies to organize this, but overall, I have found the Family Medical Leave Act to be the most important resource in my personal journey in maintaining and finding success in my roles.

Reasonable Accommodations

In the United States, the ADA plays a pivotal role in protecting employees with mental health conditions. This federal law prohibits discrimination against individuals with disabilities, including mental health disorders, in various aspects of employment, such as hiring, firing, and workplace conditions. The ADA defines a disability as "a physical or mental impairment that substantially limits one or more major life activities." This includes many mental health conditions, such as depression, anxiety, bipolar disorder, PTSD, and schizophrenia.

Under the Americans with Disabilities Act, employers are required to provide reasonable accommodations to employees with disabilities, unless doing so would cause undue hardship to the business. Reasonable accommodations can be so important for individuals to feel safe and comfortable and more successful and productive in their jobs. However, what does *reasonable accommodation* even mean?

Basically, a reasonable accommodation is an adjustment made to a role to make it fair for employees of all abilities to be able to perform the role. Examples of reasonable accommodations might include adjustments to work schedules, the ability to work remotely, or modifications to the work environment to reduce stressors.

The important word to remember is *reasonable* because not all accommodations are required from an employer or even possible for them to make, depending on the industry or specific job. Making reasonable accommodations can be difficult in certain industries, especially in fast-paced roles or jobs that require a lot of physical work.

In my own circumstances, I was able to use reasonable accommodations as a distribution center operator, as a custodian, and even in my office roles. However, the accommodations were different in each of my jobs.

- As a distribution center operator, I had a reasonable accommodation that if I started having symptoms or issues, I could help with warehouse jobs that didn't require me to be operating machinery (like labeling, cleaning, etc.). This was both for safety and to accommodate me being able to stay if symptoms were minor and didn't require me to leave work.

- As a custodian, I had a reasonable accommodation that I could listen to podcasts or music as a distraction for my schizophrenia symptoms or if I was feeling anxious. Listening to music was not allowed based on company policies, but my manager and HR manager made the adjustment for me to accommodate my symptoms and make my workday easier to get through and keep me from needing to leave or take time off as often with active symptoms.

- When I worked in an office, my reasonable accommodation was simply that I could leave the floor (where I needed to engage with customers) until I either had symptom relief and could return to work or needed to leave for the day due to symptom severity.

These are just a few examples, but finding reasonable accommodations won't be possible without discussing your needs with management and HR. I found that it is so important to communicate your needs clearly and work closely with your HR team to find accommodations that are realistic and effective. Employers are obligated to engage in an interactive process to determine the most effective accommodations that will allow you to perform your job functions without compromising your mental health.

The adjustments need to be directly related to your diagnosis or disorder. There are many examples of people with depression or anxiety being able to work from home permanently or more often as a reasonable accommodation for these symptoms. However, this becomes difficult if companies decide that what you are requesting is not reasonable for the role or not possible. This may be a telling point of whether your employer or company does not have a positive and supportive environment or culture.

It is important to know your rights as a worker. No matter what industry you work in or what state you live in, you have rights as an employee, and although some of your rights may differ based on your state legislation, certain workers' rights are federal law and required to be followed by your employer. Understanding your rights as an employee with mental health issues is crucial for ensuring you receive the proper mental health and mental illness support to perform your job effectively.

Privacy and Retaliation

To request accommodations under the ADA, I did need to disclose my mental health condition to my employer and provide documentation from my healthcare provider, which in this case was my psychiatrist.

Employees with mental health issues or mental illness diagnoses are also protected from retaliation under the ADA. This means that employers cannot punish you or treat you unfairly for requesting accommodations or utilizing programs like EAP and FMLA. Any medical information shared with an employer or HR must be kept confidential and only disclosed on a need-to-know basis, ensuring your privacy is maintained. In some of my jobs I have gone on to tell managers and coworkers about my mental health struggles, but that was my choice, and I was not required to do it. If I would have preferred that no one else knew, that was also my right to have that privacy under the ADA.

In addition, the company, your manager, and your co-workers cannot retaliate in any way for you utilizing any of these mental health resources. There have been cases in the past in which companies have been found guilty of retaliation and ADA discrimination for trying to punish or firing employees for disclosing a disability (including mental illnesses and mental health issues) or using services like FMLA.

If you believe that a company is trying to retaliate because of time off, use of FMLA, or use of reasonable accommodations, be sure to document it and address it. If a manager or coworker harasses or discriminates against a person for any of these reasons, this needs to be documented and reported to the employer to address immediately.

If the employer or company refuses to address these issues or continues to retaliate, you may have to seek further guidance with the Equal Employment Opportunity Commission or even an employment/ADA lawyer.

In addition to reasonable accommodations, FMLA, and EAP, there are other resources that you can look into in the workplace. Some workplaces will invest in additional mental health resources. Be sure that you ask about what your company has for mental health resources if they do not cover it in your new hire orientation. I have worked at places that won't ever acknowledge mental health, and I've also worked at companies that took it upon themselves to start mental health initiatives in the workplace.

Thankfully, more companies are seeing employees express a need for mental health awareness and resources and are following through with providing more in order to retain those employees. In Chapters 11 and 12, I will discuss options that employers can provide outside of the typical mental health services to go above and beyond for their employees' mental health and well-being. We are seeing positive changes in the workplace for mental health, but even if companies embrace mental health, employees will need to take it upon themselves to learn to unmask and set boundaries at work to preserve their own mental health and stability.

I have unfortunately had many negative experiences that led to me trying to hide my struggles or emotions as a way to ensure that I would not be discriminated against or lose

opportunities within the company. However, it is important to know that behavior came at a cost of worsening
mental health and eventual burnout. It is important to see
the cost associated with trying to mask in the workplace,
something we'll talk about in the next chapter.

Chapter 6

Unmasking and Setting Boundaries

After starting to manage my mental health at work, one of the most challenging things about beginning to be myself again was learning to unmask.

For many years I masked how I was feeling because I didn't want to be talked about or lose opportunities, so I had to relearn how to be myself and not change the way I acted to please others. I knew that when I was doing well, I was a good worker, and I was proud of my productivity and commitment to my company. It was difficult to come in every day and put on a performance to make everyone I worked with believe I was happy and doing well. Trying to maintain this façade would constantly put me into burnout, which would inevitably lead to me taking more time off work or even losing my job.

What specifically do I mean by masking and unmasking? *Masking* is a behavior in which a person hides what they are feeling in fear of being judged. The act of masking is very common for people struggling with mental illness and is also a common behavior in people who are neurodivergent and on the autism spectrum. Therefore, *unmasking* is a process in which someone has to learn how to

67

not "camouflage" themselves after doing so for a period of time and instead act in a genuine matter.

Unmasking may just seem like the act of "not masking," but people who mask emotions, traits of neurodivergence, and mental health issues don't usually make a *conscious* decision to do so. Oftentimes, masking is an act of self-preservation, a trauma response, or an unconscious way to "fit in" or conform to social pressures. Most people mask because they do not feel safe showing their real emotions or personality either at work, in public, or at home with certain friends or family.

So the process of unmasking requires more than just not masking. It requires you to:

- **Be aware that you are masking.** This may be a shock to learn, but did you know that not everyone is even aware that they are masking? I found this in my own journey and with many mental health advocates who may have experienced trauma or abuse (not just physical but verbal or psychological abuse too) from a young age. People who started masking at a young age tend to do so as a form of survival, not intentionally, and are often unaware that they are masking. As mentioned, this is also common in people on the autism spectrum, who mask as a way to feel more accepted by mirroring "normal" behaviors. Recognizing that you may be masking is the first step to unmasking.

- **Address the reasons why you may have started masking in the first place.** The next step is to figure out who, or what, made you feel like you had to mask your emotions or mental health struggles in the first place. In my own journey with unmasking, I realized that I masked at work because of the work ethic that was instilled in me by my grandpa and the environment of the rural area I grew up in, as I discussed in Chapter 1. With no one around me ever acknowledging mental health or burnout, I figured that was just a regular thing that I needed to deal with, which kept me from getting help. It can be easier to unmask if you can address the person or situation(s) that led to feeling unsafe to be your authentic self.

- **Feel safe enough to start unmasking.** In some situations, the person or environment that led to masking may still be a part of your life. In that case, unmasking can be that much more challenging, especially if you feel unsafe by showing certain emotions or talking about mental health. If possible, it may be more productive to find separation from stressors before trying to unmask. It is important to feel safe and accepted while learning to be your authentic self, so try to surround yourself with people who embrace your efforts to unmask your emotions and mental health.

- **Be willing to accept that some people may not like you unmasked.** I found that when I stopped masking and acted more based on my mental health state, some of my friends and coworkers did not like it. They had been around me only in times where I was pretending to be okay, so when I was more open about my feelings and mental health, they either stopped interacting with me or started avoiding me completely. I tried to rebuild some of those relationships, only to realize that those people never liked me or my personality – only the fictional personality I created in order to be liked. It is likely that you will encounter similar experiences with people around you. I would prefer to surround myself with people who can understand my mental health or my mental illness and are comfortable with me discussing them openly.

- **Be stable enough in your mental health to be consistent with it.** If you are going through a big life change or have any situational stressors, it may be beneficial to wait before trying to start unmasking. I found that it was easier to start learning to unmask when I had adequate time and energy so that I could get used to doing it each day. I found if I made it a habit, I wouldn't find myself falling back into masking when I was back in burnout.

- **Remember that this process may not be linear.** It is okay to start unmasking in small ways to make yourself more comfortable. This process does not have to be all or nothing. Take things at your own pace, and remember that it is okay to have setbacks too. This process may look different for everyone.

I was incredibly nervous to start being myself around my coworkers. After getting my diagnosis and my medication, I spent years trying to make everyone around me believe I was stable and not continuing to struggle with mental health issues. The problem with trying to mask my emotions is that some weeks I spent more time with my coworkers than I did with my family, especially when I was working in production, manufacturing, and distribution in jobs that required a lot of overtime throughout the year. It even became difficult to express myself at home because I would spend so much time at work pretending to be someone else.

Unmasking at work can be a long process, especially if you are doing it in a role that you have been in for years. People are used to you acting a certain way based on experiences they have while working with you, so if you try to change that and start setting boundaries or acting "differently," it can be noticeable.

In the first company that I decided to try unmasking and acting how I really felt, it was so stressful because almost every coworker I spoke to was bringing up how I didn't seem as happy as usual and announcing it to everyone. Masking for me comes off very animated and energetic. When I tried to unmask in a workplace that I had worked at for almost a full year, everyone noticed. I tried unmasking for a full week, but I went back to masking because everyone made a big show out of me not being overly energetic. Acknowledging and expressing my struggles was a critical step toward healing. It allowed me to process my emotions more openly and reduce the burden of hiding it constantly.

A perfect time to try unmasking is when starting a new job or joining a new company because your new coworkers won't know the difference. I tried unmasking again when I took a new job a few months later. I was able to act in a way that was least "performative," and although my natural personality is a bit more animated than most, it is still far from my masking personality. Waiting to unmask until I came to my new job was much easier, and by the time I had met all my coworkers, I was able to mostly overcome my masking.

I know that some people worry about not being considered for new opportunities or promotions. I worried about this a lot when I started setting boundaries for my mental health. I also worried about my coworkers thinking negatively about me or talking about me behind my back. This will again be something to consider before completely unmasking, but having an already open line of communication may be a way to avoid some of this concern.

When I tried unmasking by refusing to work an additional 6 hours after a 12-hour shift because another employee called in sick, my shift manager responded, "You really need to be more of a team player." This was also while I was greatly struggling with anxiety that was causing me to get very little sleep at night. I knew that I physically could not do it, but I had done such a good job masking in the past and not setting boundaries that I had worked many additional shifts in the past – even earlier that same week!

This was a job where I hadn't told anyone about my diagnosis yet, but I was so frustrated that he would try to guilt trip me when I had never said no to working overtime before. I decided to try to be honest because I felt bad, and

I told him that I was very tired, stressed, and anxious lately. He told me that I would never be able to become a manager if I didn't "get over [my] bullshit from [my] home life" because I was not chosen for a lead position the previous week for the second time.

Interactions like this are what prevent people with good work ethic from asking for help. No one wants to be an inconvenience. No one wants to be considered not a team player. I wanted to feel like part of the team and to be engaged in the work I was doing. I felt like I gave so much effort to this job, but my trying to set reasonable boundaries made this manager think that I was not a good worker and didn't care about my job. If this is how he reacted from my simply turning down an overtime shift, how would he react if I tried to go to him about my health or safety?

After that experience with my manager, I started masking again and stopped trying to set boundaries. I didn't want to disappoint anyone, and I didn't want to feel like I couldn't do my job. So, I went back to not advocating for myself and hiding my struggles, only to end up burning myself out again. After a few months, I crashed. I ended up having to admit myself to the hospital for several mental health issues and taking time off, which resulted in me almost losing my job again. I felt useless. I felt like I couldn't keep up with anyone else, and when I tried to be honest about that, I was treated poorly.

It is also important to acknowledge that masking looks different for everyone. I mentioned that for me, masking was pretending to be more outgoing and energetic. It can be common for people to pretend to be more social, lively, or conversational in an attempt to fit in with peers. Meanwhile, for others, masking may look more like withdrawing from social situations or being less willing to make small talk. Masking is just any individual's way of camouflaging mental health or neurodivergence in an attempt to feel more "normal" or neurotypical. Although the term *masking* is most commonly used for autism or ADHD, it can refer to other mental health conditions too.

In the same way that masking can look different for many people, so can *unmasking*. Because masking can be both a conscious and unconscious set of behaviors, some individuals may not even realize that what they are doing *is* unmasking. This was the case for me; as I started to set boundaries (both at work and in my personal life), stopped pretending to be so energetic to match the energy of the people around me, and started to ask for help when I needed it, I was unknowingly starting to unmask. Unmasking and being myself made it possible for me to gain the support of my coworkers, management, and even HR at this job.

It is so crucial to surround yourself with people who understand your needs and are willing to support you if you experience low periods. The most effective way to do this is to make sure you are surrounding yourself with positive people both at work and in your personal life as well. Being around understanding and empathetic people makes it so much easier to stop masking, set boundaries, and be your authentic self. If you don't have support at home or in your personal life, it can be very difficult to set boundaries at work. The people in my personal life are the ones who communicated the importance of not over-working myself and starting to prioritize self-care, something we'll talk about in Chapter 8.

Even if you feel comfortable setting personal boundaries and unmasking in your personal life, it can still be challenging to implement this at work. The question I always ask to management teams when I speak with employers across the country is "Why do you think workers are afraid to set boundaries?"

The answer is because employees are afraid that they will miss out on promotions and other opportunities just for addressing mental health or setting basic boundaries that they need to be able to thrive at work. In a perfect world, no one would miss out on a promotion or advancement opportunity for having mental health struggles, but it is a very real concern that a person may not get a job because management knows that they struggle with depression or some other diagnosis. Unmasking can carry risks such as facing discrimination or misunderstanding from colleagues or supervisors. It is important to weigh these risks and consider the workplace culture before making the decision to unmask.

In addition to missing out on jobs or opportunities, everyone wants to feel accepted and included at work. I saw in my own experience that in certain jobs, people would stop talking to me or involving me for talking about my diagnosis or trying to have conversation about mental health at work.

I didn't let that stop me from discussing these things, but it was always frustrating to notice that some people would think differently about me simply because my brain functions differently than theirs and I was vocal about my mental health. I would eventually find people that were more able to articulate and discuss similar experiences, but I did feel very isolated when I first started opening up. I realized that was okay because did I really want to maintain friendships with people who didn't support me or even know what I was really like?

Unmasking led to people wanting to spend less time with me, sometimes not even engaging with me at all. I know that is what many people fear with being their authentic selves, and it is likely you will lose people from your life who are not willing to accommodate you, learn about your illness or struggles, or even accept you for acting differently than when you masked. I know that can be hard to hear, but the positive news is that unmasking and being your true self will lead you to more likeminded, accepting, and accommodating people who will make your life more fulfilling and easier.

While I was starting to explore mental health in the workplace as a topic for this book, I was speaking to a former coworker from the job I had at the manufacturing facility, and he asked, "If unmasking and setting boundaries is so difficult and it could possibly lead to missing opportunities, or feeling isolated, why even do it?"

I explained, "It was better to do it early on because eventually I would not have a choice."

He looked at me with confusion, so I explained, "Masking was a temporary fix. Not setting boundaries could only last so long. These were short-term solutions for an unresolved issue. There is a reason that I worked in so many different jobs and industries and why I couldn't hold jobs as long as my peers. It is because I could pretend to be fine and functional but only for so long. Eventually my declining mental health would catch up, and I would need to either leave my job or I would get fired. It was only a matter of time before I would fall into burnout."

Which prompted this question from him: "What is burnout?"

That leads us nicely into the next chapter, which is about burnouts and breakdowns and how you can watch for the signs of them and try to avoid them altogether.

Chapter 7

Burnouts and Breakdowns
Seeing the Signs

I have lost several jobs because of burnout. I have been both fired and forced to quit because I was no longer able to do a job I had done for months or even years. Burnout can happen to both neurodivergent and neurotypical people; it can happen to people with or without mental illness too. Burnout is a state of mental, physical, and emotional exhaustion that can be caused by chronic or prolonged stress. It is often associated with work-related stress. Although many people assume that burnout is exclusive to mental illness or developmental disabilities like autism, it is actually possible for anyone who is stressed or overworked for long periods of time to get overwhelmed to the point of burnout.

Tips for Recognizing Burnout

According to a 2024 NAMI poll, more than half (52%) of employees reported feeling burned out in the past year because of their job, and 37% reported feeling so overwhelmed it made it hard for them to do their job.[1] Those

---

[1] https://www.nami.org/support-education/publications-reports/survey-reports/the-2024-nami-workplace-mental-health-poll

numbers should really express the need to discuss mental health and setting boundaries with employers. When more than half of workers are reporting feeling burned out because of their jobs, employers need to start reevaluating workloads, hiring more staff, and looking at other options to help employees.

In many cases, workers may look for other jobs if they feel that the workplace is causing negative mental health issues. Millennials and Gen Z already leave jobs and transfer jobs more frequently than other generations, and based on conversations with other mental health advocates, it is commonly due to employees feeling so burned out that they did not have any other choice but to leave and find something more accommodating.

This could be seen during the COVID-19 pandemic, with what some called the "Great Resignation" or the "Big Quit." The Great Resignation was a period of time during COVID-19 that employees voluntarily resigned from their jobs, many of whom changed companies and some even industries. Many employees reported leaving because of hostile/toxic work environments, inflexible remote work accommodations, and overall frustration with a job or company. This is a hopeful sign that employees are putting mental health first and leaving to find more accommodating workplaces.

With more than half of employees reporting feeling burned out in the last year, it seems that although more companies than ever claim to care about employee mental health (and even use mental health resources as a recruiting talking point), employees are not maintaining a positive work-life balance. Employers need to look at what they can do beyond just having an EAP and actually take mental health initiatives. I will talk more about the role of employers and leadership in promoting positive mental health, but I want to start with how employees can recognize burnout and what coping mechanisms may be useful in preventing burnout.

Burnout can look different for everyone but there are some common signs that you can look out for: decreased productivity, exhaustion, feelings of hopelessness, sleep changes or irregularities, depression, anxiety, social isolation, and more. There are so many burnout symptoms that can greatly affect a person's ability to not just work but function day to day. There are also many job-related reasons why someone may feel burned out. Burnout can often be attributed to:

- Feeling a lack of control
- Problems managing responsibilities
- Misleading or misunderstood expectations for the role
- Issues with coworkers or management
- Displeasure with workplace environment/culture
- Being overworked (often due to workplace understaffing)
- Feeling excluded, alone, or isolated

These are just a few examples of things that can lead to burnout. I found that in order to prevent burnout, I needed to focus on identifying triggers like these and understanding the needed self-care to align with these triggers. This can look different for everyone depending on what mental health issues or mental illness symptoms they most commonly struggle with, how they cope, what their care team looks like (if they have one at all), and how comfortable they are reaching out for help. Not everyone will experience triggers, but those who experience recurring mental health decline or burnout might start to notice patterns of things associated with these low periods.

Basically, a *trigger* is a stimulus that elicits a reaction. It can be an event or situation that can bring on or worsen symptoms. It is often used in association with people with histories of mental illness, self-harm, trauma, or addiction. Many things can be a trigger for someone to experience worsened symptoms. Identifying triggers in yourself can be an effective way to be cautious and immediately address situations that could bring on symptoms.

In my own experience, trying to mask in the workplace, being overworked due to understaffing, and dealing with job stress have been the most common causes of burnout. Burnout should be discussed more often with tips on how to avoid it. Over the years, I have found different coping mechanisms that help to avoid burnout.

Tips for Avoiding Burnout

These are the most important tips I have used for avoiding burnout:

- **Practice self-care:** Self-care can look different for everyone, and it may take time to find what works best for you. Prioritizing sleep and physical activity were the two forms of self-care that helped me the most. A lack of sleep greatly affected my ability to work, maintain proper hygiene, and even be engaged in activities in my personal life. Not being active caused me to be more fatigued and irritable throughout the day. Focusing on these acts of self-care made it possible for me to get through each day with more energy, more positivity, and less concern of falling into burnout. For me, that means keeping a regular sleep schedule, avoiding isolation, eating healthy, and more.

- **Be willing to ask for help:** The 2024 NAMI Workplace Mental Health Poll[2] shows that employees who are less comfortable talking about their mental health at work are more likely to report feeling burnout and their mental health suffering because of work. As I have discussed, reaching out for help can be incredibly difficult, but if you are experiencing signs of burnout, it is so important to ask for help as soon as you identify the need for it. I have reached out for help to my wife, my mother, my psychiatrist, my manager, and many more. What kind of help do you ask for? It depends on what you need. When I just needed someone to vent to, I would talk to my wife. If I needed guidance on a decision, I would talk to my mother. If I was having symptoms that concerned me, I would set up an appointment with my psychiatrist. Having good communication with my care team kept

---

[2] https://www.nami.org/support-education/publications-reports/survey-reports/the-2024-nami-workplace-mental-health-poll

me from dwelling on negative mental health that may have led to burnout.

- **Avoid self-isolation:** When someone is experiencing signs of burnout or issues with mental health, it is common to self-isolate and avoid people and social events. A lack of social interaction can have negative psychological impacts. I withdrew from my friends, family, and peers many times while struggling with mental health issues. Although I thought it was helpful in the moment, I know now that it was just a way for me to not have to acknowledge or discuss anything I was dealing with. In-person and online peer support groups allowed me to start talking about different topics of concern while keeping me from not interacting with others during low points.

- **Educate yourself about mental health:** Better understanding of mental health, mental illness, and burnout made me feel more in control of my ability to prevent burnout. I knew what signs or symptoms to look out for and when I should be concerned enough to ask for help. Education on topics like this also made it easier for me to correct people who were a part of misleading or untrue conversations about mental health, which made those around me more knowledgeable, understanding, and empathetic to myself and others who may require certain assistance or accommodations. Knowing more about my mental health led to less stigma in the workplace and to me even being asked to help lead employee mental health initiatives at work. (See the "Resources" at the end of the book for some places to start.)

- **Find hobbies outside of work:** Having a strong work ethic or being proud of the work you do can sometimes make people forget that there is life outside of work. Even if you love your job and are passionate about the job, it is so important to find a good work-life balance. Not having hobbies or goals outside of work can be another way to find yourself in burnout. I realized this when I was working in an office job for my college. I found the work very interesting, and I was passionate about it, but I stopped focusing on my life outside of work and found myself struggling to keep up when I was there. Whether it is hiking, painting, or sports, find time to relax and engage with nonwork activities.

- **Use your time off:** Some companies and managers made me feel bad or guilty about using my time off. This is unacceptable and extremely toxic workplace behavior. While working in certain jobs, I knew other employees who took pride in never using their allotted time off and never calling in sick. These same employees would seem to struggle the most in the long run with mental health and physical illness too. Companies use time off as a way to recruit workers, and it is meant to be there for employees to use as needed. Be sure to use your time off as needed for mental health days or to focus on hobbies or time with family. If you find yourself needing more than what is allotted, you can start looking into companies with more paid time off, or you can pursue FMLA for unpaid time off if needed for an ongoing health issue.

- **Focus on physical health improvements:** When I got to a point of stability with my mental health, I found that maintaining my physical health helped me stay out of burnout longer. I will acknowledge that it took a while for me to feel comfortable enough with my diagnosis and mental health before I could work on my physical health. Having a gym routine, healthier diet, and more frequent health checkups may not cure your mental health issues – like some people may suggest – but can be an excellent addition to mental health maintenance alongside medication and other treatment options.

- **Set goals (start small):** I still make a to-do list every single day. Some people find it silly that the first two items on my list of goals each day are "wake up" and "get out of bed." A friend asked why I had to write those down. "Isn't that common sense? That's how everyone starts their day." I had to explain that in times that I am struggling, those have been the only tasks I could complete, and some days I couldn't even do that. Negative mental health can affect your motivation and your ability to take care of yourself. By setting small goals, I found that I felt some accomplishment just from completing these goals, and that gave me a sense of hope that I could add more and more goals to the list and get through each day feeling more accomplished.

To-do lists can make you feel accomplished, and by keeping the goals small, you can achieve a sense of accomplishment to help you get through the day. But make sure to use what tool works for you – you don't need fancy software or a hyper-featured app. Sometimes just simple pen and paper are best. And remember to start small and stay steady. You don't want your to-do list to lead you back to burnout.

These are all tips that have helped me feel more comfortable and successful in the workplace.

It's Not Just You: Everyone Needs to Set Boundaries

Before I knew about triggers or had any of these tips for preventing burnout, I was constantly faced with two options: keep trying to mask until I found myself in a hospital or stop masking that I was struggling and get fired for not being able to keep up with my peers. Even if I loved the job or my coworkers, it would eventually get to a point where I could not manage my mental health anymore and end up in burnout. From conversations with advocates, I found this was common not just for mental health advocates but for autism advocates and other neurodivergent individuals as well.

People that I spoke to on the autism spectrum shared this same frustration with constant struggles with burnout, even more so because neurodivergent individuals tend to experience burnout more frequently due to overstimulating work environments and needing to constantly interact with people. This also leads to individuals with autism being more likely to be unemployed and unable to work. I have been able to work with many autism advocates who can confirm this, but I have also known this to be true as a caregiver for and spouse to a person on the autism spectrum. Although all of the topics in this book can be relevant to people that are neurodivergent, I have seen my wife, Allyson, deal with burnout from many types of employment including serving, production, and various types of office roles.

Allyson didn't receive her diagnoses of autism and ADHD until she was almost 30 years old. She had struggled all her life with sensory issues, meltdowns, difficulties navigating social interactions, and maintaining personal relationships. All of these issues, alongside mental health struggles, make maintaining a job very difficult and have often led to such severe burnout that it would manifest into physical health issues. Studies (listed at https://mydisabilityjobs.com/statistics/autism-employment/) estimate that 85% of people with autism are unemployed for these very reasons. Workplaces with rigid policies that are unable to be accommodating make it nearly impossible for neurodivergent individuals to find success in employment.

She says, "I really never set boundaries until my most recent job, largely because I didn't have an autism diagnosis until last year. The most effective boundaries I established at work were getting approved for FMLA, actually using my FMLA benefits, and knowing my rights involved with taking time off. This included not volunteering to make up the time just because I felt guilty because I needed this time off to prevent burnout."

I use this example to remind anyone reading that regardless of whether you have a schizophrenia diagnosis, a mental illness, symptoms of depression; are a neurodivergent person; or have negative mental health issues, you too can experience burnout. Although the severity and the longevity of burnout may be different for each person, it is so important to acknowledge that it can happen to anyone. Without setting boundaries, you may also find yourself in burnout.

What to Do If You Do Burn Out

If you do find yourself in burnout, try to remember that there *are* options outside of being fired or leaving your job – especially if you have already talked to HR or management about any mental health concerns or diagnosis you may have.

- **Discuss your concerns with HR:** If you have already disclosed your concerns with HR and have open communication with them, this is usually an effective first step as they may recommend some of the other options I've listed or might even offer job-specific accommodations or resources.
- **Seek professional help:** If you have healthcare and the means to speak to a professional, this may be the best way to address burnout. If a mental health

professional is unable to provide insight or assistance, they should at least be able to help you get the proper paperwork that your employer would need to get reasonable accommodations or even temporary adjustment of your workload.

- **Adjust your workload and responsibilities:** It may not always be an option, but it is worth speaking with your employer to see about adjusting your workload and responsibilities. This might include delegating tasks, prioritizing projects, or setting more realistic deadlines. Based on my own experience and in speaking with my peers, I know this can be difficult depending on the employer and industry you work in.

- **Consider flexible work arrangements:** Flexible work arrangements, such as remote work, flexible hours, or part-time schedules, can reduce stress and improve work-life balance. I was able to transition to part-time hours in a previous role while returning to college, and that made me less stressed and more productive while at work. Remote work may be the biggest consideration for flexible work arrangements as the world continues to become more online and digital. Again, this will largely depend on your employer's willingness to find a solution and ability to accommodate these changes.

- **Develop healthy work habits:** Implementing healthy work habits, such as taking regular breaks, setting boundaries between work and personal life, and organizing your workspace, can help manage stress levels.

- **Join support groups:** Support groups, both within your community and online, can be a way to feel supported, less isolated, and less alone in your mental health journey. NAMI has both online support groups as well as in-person groups for mental health all over the country. Joining peer support groups gave me more hope and inspiration than any other option for dealing with burnout and understanding my ongoing struggles with mental health.

- **Consider career counseling:** Career counseling can help you evaluate your current job situation and explore other career options if your current role is contributing significantly to your burnout. Some employers offer this option, and it is something that I have done at a company to apply for and transition to a position that would be able to better accommodate both my personal and mental health needs. See the "Resources" section at the end of the book for more information.

- **Evaluate your long-term goals:** It can be hard to admit that a career or job may not be a good fit for you. I have had to reevaluate my career choices in the past when I was finding myself in constant burnout. This was the main reason for my transition from labor-based jobs to office-based jobs. I realized that although I did enjoy some of these industries, the work environments and job tasks were not compatible with my mental illness or mental health issues. Sometimes, making a complete career change or shifting to a different role within the same company can alleviate burnout. It is important to not look at this like failing but as an opportunity to find success and fulfillment in a new job or industry.

- **Practice self-care:** Incorporating self-care activities into your daily routine, such as exercise, meditation, hobbies, and adequate sleep, can work either as a way to prevent burnout or help pull you out of burnout.

By exploring and implementing these options, you can try to preemptively address mental health burnout and move toward a healthier work-life balance. Although it was very hard for me to stay employed once I reached burn-out, it was largely because I had usually not talked with my employer beforehand and was too embarrassed by the time I reached burnout. I often just accepted that I would either be let go or would need to leave to find a new job. Now I know that I can talk with HR to look at other options, ask my care team for advice or resources, reevaluate my goals, and continue to prioritize self-care, which we'll talk all about in the next chapter.

Chapter 8

Self-Care for the 9-to-5 Grind

Self-care can mean a lot of different things. Everyone will have their own version of taking care of themselves to prevent declining mental health or prevent burnout. No matter what industry you work in, what type of job you have, or if you work mornings or overnights, you can fall into burnout if you don't take preemptive measures to care for yourself.

What Is Self-Care?

Although I can't list every single option for self-care in this chapter, I can share what has been effective for me in taking care of myself both at work and at home. While reading this chapter, remember that self-care does not have a one-size-fits-all approach; it is about finding what works best for you and integrating those practices into your routine. This is similar to how two people may have the same diagnosis but need different medications to treat it.

When people hear the term *self-care*, many might think it is only referring to your mental well-being, but it is actually referencing your *overall* well-being. There are different pillars of self-care:

- Physical
- Environmental
- Emotional
- Mental
- Social
- Spiritual
- Professional

There are ways to have a balanced care routine, and it can be important to consider all the pillars instead of focusing on just one. I will discuss the importance of self-care in the workplace, break down each pillar of self-care, reveal what types of care are common for those pillars, and explain which self-care techniques were most effective in my own mental health journey.

Self-care is the practice of taking an active role to preserve or protect one's own health, well-being, and happiness, especially during periods of stress. With more than half of workers reporting feeling burned out in the last year because of work, and knowing that work is the primary cause of burnout, focusing on taking care of yourself in the workplace is more important than ever. Workplace stress, in my opinion, is inevitable. Even if you love your job, company, and mission, you can still experience stress.

I have had some level of stress in every job I've ever had – even in the roles that I have been extremely excited and passionate about. Sometimes I would be *more* stressed in jobs that I enjoyed because I would put more pressure on myself to do a good job and make a difference. I don't think you can have a job without some varying levels of stress. The most effective way to deal with that stress is by focusing on some form of self-care. Identifying the stressor can help determine what self-care options may work best for you.

Occupational or work-related stress can be attributed to many factors like workplace relationships, constant change, and a lack of control. Not being able to make decisions about your environment, rules and policies, and the people you work with every day can be frustrating. There have been jobs where I have been stuck working with coworkers who have judged me for my mental health issues, and I've had to continue to see them and interact with them daily. I had a coworker tell me that I was "just weak" for calling in for mental health reasons, and I worked with him every day for over a year.

It was also stressful knowing that every day I came into work that the company might change a policy or rule that could completely change my job or daily schedule, and I would have to just accept it. These things were out of my control. I couldn't control the changes my company made or the people I worked with. The only thing I was able to have control of was how I dealt with these different stressors, and that was through self-care.

I have been able to utilize self-care in past roles to keep myself from experiencing burnout. While working in my very first job in high school, I found ways to balance school and work while maintaining my mental health. At the time, I didn't realize that I was doing self-care or trying to maintain my mental well-being. I just made an effort to go for daily walks, find time to draw or paint, and even make to-do lists to reduce stress and organize my responsibilities.

I wouldn't recognize this as self-care until well into adulthood when trying to relearn how to avoid burnout as an adult. Somehow, I was able to start taking care of myself instinctively while working a fast-food job in high school. I find this interesting as a mental health advocate and someone who has spent my entire adult life trying to understand mental health. I was just reacting to the stress of working, going to school, and being a caregiver with activities that I found healing and relaxing, almost stumbling into self-care.

Physical

The first pillar of self-care I will discuss is physical self-care. This involves activities that improve your physical health and energy levels. Incorporating physical activity into my schedule helped, even if it was a short walk at lunch. I know that people with mental health issues and mental illness can sometimes struggle with this pillar because it can be so challenging to even get out of bed some days. I knew there were days I would probably not be able to keep this habit, but I could always start again when I was out of burnout. I also found that when I was able to focus more on physical self-care that I would see additional improvements in my mental health too.

Eating healthy, exercising, getting adequate sleep, and staying hydrated are other ways that people can focus on physical self-care. I wish I could say that I have been able to implement all of these in my own life, but I have struggled with all of these. I try to keep all of them in mind when I start noticing my physical health declining. Finding ways to make this part of your daily routine can have a very positive impact. I have been able to find small ways to make sure I stay active, which can be especially important if you have a job that is less active, behind a desk, or work from home.

I found that walking was a physical activity that was not as intense or overwhelming as a full workout or going to a gym, so I started using short walks throughout my day, just to move around a bit. I immediately noticed more motivation, fewer aches and pains, better sleep at night, and more enthusiasm to add other physical activities on days I was feeling well. I also found that short bike rides and swimming were a nice way to improve my physical health and daily mood. Finding any way to be active is a win. This form of self-care doesn't have to be scary or unreasonable; just find something that works for you!

Environmental

Environmental wellness or self-care is the practice of taking care of your environment. This can be decluttering your living space, walking in nature, or exploring somewhere you've never been. I personally find that improving my living space helps me feel an achievement of completing a task and also creates a more welcoming safe space to focus on self-care.

There are many examples of ways I focus on my environment, which can be organizing my office, adding houseplants, rearranging furniture, changing air filters, and much more. I personally find myself rearranging my office frequently as a way to change my scenery and get rid of things I don't need anymore.

Emotional

The next pillar of self-care is emotional self-care. It focuses on managing and expressing your emotions in healthy ways. One of the most recommended ways to improve emotional self-care is meditation. Although I do not personally practice meditation, it has been widely discussed in this area. I personally have found success in using mindfulness and journaling to be able to ground myself, express my thoughts, and work through difficult emotions.

Engaging in hobbies can be another way to focus on emotional self-care. Again, this will look different for everyone. My hobbies include hiking, playing video games, and listening to podcasts. My hobbies are the best way for me to feel relaxed and work through any challenging times. One of the problems with adulthood is that between work and other responsibilities, it can be hard to find time to do our hobbies. I urge you to make time to paint, crochet, go fishing, or do any hobbies that give you relief and relaxation.

Some people I know have implemented a social aspect to their emotional self-care activities. Social isolation can be very damaging to a person's cognitive and behavioral functioning, so finding ways to have time for connecting with someone can be important. This doesn't have to be going out or a big event. This could be a phone call with a friend, conversation and coffee, or even a short walk with someone to catch up. (See also "Social," coming up.)

Mental

Next is mental self-care. This pillar may be the most relevant in my stories and discussions about mental health and mental illness. This pillar involves activities that stimulate your mind and promote cognitive well-being. For me, the most helpful aspects of maintaining mental self-care are continuous learning and making to-do lists. Continuous learning can be everything from learning a new language to taking challenging classes or even just listening to a podcast about a topic that interests you. The idea is to keep the brain engaged and prevent cognitive issues.

Making to-do lists and focusing on time management have been great ways for me to set new goals, improve my memory, and find ways to have more time for hobbies and new goals. Aside from continuous learning and setting goals, many advocates also recommend a "digital detox." Although a large part of my career is social media content creation, even I recognize the importance of taking breaks from technology and social media.

Social

The next pillar is social self-care, and it involves building and maintaining healthy relationships and social connections. I would do this by making friends at work. However, not everyone wants to intertwine their personal and professional lives. So, a few other options would be to join local groups or clubs that you are interested in, find volunteer opportunities, and work on spending time with family or already established friends. I know when I was struggling with my mental health, building and maintaining relationships was extremely challenging. A common symptom of burnout and mental illness is self-isolation, but isolation can be one of the worst things for someone struggling with declining mental health.

Spiritual

Another pillar is spiritual self-care, and it involves focusing your spiritual or religious beliefs and practices. This can be through joining a spiritual or religious community, meditating, or connecting with nature. The idea is to create a sense of belonging and strengthen an individual's sense of self.

Professional

The final pillar is the professional self-care pillar. I saved this for last because it is the most relevant in talking about self-care in the workplace. I have felt the most fulfilled in a professional setting when I have been able to have a realistic work-life balance, set career goals, use my PTO and vacation time, and seek ways to invest in my professional development. If you are looking into setting career goals, it is okay to remember that those can change over time and with new knowledge and experiences.

I found myself trying new industries and working at new companies until I could find a professional role that best fit my mental health needs and allowed me to still pursue advocacy for schizophrenia and mental illness awareness, which eventually would become my full-time profession.

I personally have found the most success in the workplace by practicing mindfulness, making time for my hobbies outside of work, finding coping mechanisms for work and home, having a plan for times of struggle, focusing on preventative care instead of emergency care, and prioritizing rest and sleep. These are just a few examples of self-care activities that helped me during times of declining mental health or times of increased schizophrenia symptoms. Much of my self-care at work revolved around identifying my times of need and finding ways to prevent worsened mental health.

Preventative Self-Care

I think one of the most important factors of self-care, and also the least discussed, is taking *preventative* self-care measures. Many people try to focus on self-care *after* they start to notice a pattern of declining mental health or once they have fallen into burnout.

I always assumed my grandfather could never understand mental health or burnout because he was a hard-working, career-long tradesman who never spoke openly about his emotions or mental health, but I once told him about an issue I was having at work, and he said to me, "Companies always wait to repair equipment until it is broken down, when they could save a lot of time, energy, and resources by investing in preventative maintenance instead. Doesn't make much sense, does it? Yet people will do the same to themselves constantly."

I think about this a lot – not just because it is a great analogy but because it changed my perspective on mental health, people with different life experiences, and how I may have my own unconscious bias of certain people.

As I mentioned earlier, I didn't expect my grandfather to understand mental health let alone have such insight on it. I realized that I had assumed this with other people in my life based on where they lived and what they did for work. I realized that just because someone doesn't talk about mental health doesn't mean they don't understand it or even have their own ways of coping and prioritizing self-care. Although my grandpa may have had very different ways of focusing on his own self-care, it was clear he had thought about the importance of planning ahead.

Some of the ways that I have focused on "preventative maintenance" in the workplace is by having those early conversations with my employer. By letting them know about my diagnosis beforehand, I avoid having to document or have these conversations in crisis. I also let people in my care team know what the best ways are to help me if I fall into burnout or have obvious signs of mental health decline. This makes it easier for my wife, friends, and even coworkers to reach out with concerns and have the tools needed to help me get back on track. Lastly, I try to find different coping mechanisms for dealing with negative mental health issues or symptoms of my schizophrenia. Having these mechanisms allows me to ground myself and feel more safe and secure.

Self-care is a time investment, and frankly it can be time-consuming. It does require making time to focus on some of the activities described in this chapter. I have neglected my self-care in the past to take on more overtime or an additional part-time job. We all have bills to pay. But it always ends in burnout. It took me many years to realize working so much might make me more money, but it will never be worth the amount of stress it causes, the lack of sleep I get, or the eventual burnout I will find myself in.

"You worked 80 hours last week? Well, I worked over 100 hours last week!"

If you have ever worked in a manual-labor job, you've probably heard conversations like this. I remember people I worked with in manual labor jobs constantly bragging and being proud of working double what the average American worked in a week. I found myself doing this as well. I remember bragging about working 28 days in a row of 12-hour shifts while employed at a factory, or a full 7-day work week of 16-hour shifts in a distribution plant when overtime was required. I was so proud that I could work so much, but it didn't benefit me in any way other than a slightly bigger paycheck.

I was working so much that I stopped doing *any* type of self-care. I was constantly exhausted and in pain, and I realized that this was what most of the men in these industries did all of the time. Some extra money on my paycheck was not worth the time I lost with my friends and family or the hours of additional stress I put on my mind and body. But that seemed normal for the people who worked in these jobs. Not implementing preventative self-care was causing me way more mental health issues and burnout, but at the time I had not started addressing these issues and had no idea how much it was affecting my mental health.

Neither employers nor employees should be promoting or glorifying overworking, and although I specifically mentioned my experience in manual labor to discuss overworking, this applies to all industries and types of employment. I have seen a correlation in workplaces that glorify overworking and workplaces with the highest turnover. Working too many hours leaves no time for self-care, setting goals, or a life outside of work. If you are an employer, *promoting* a work-life balance for your employees will ensure a more positive, engaged, and sustainable working environment for everyone and will help prevent a constant need to have to rehire. If you are an employee, *having* a work-life balance will lead to a more fulfilling life outside of work and allow you to focus on being a well-rounded human being.

By addressing your physical, environmental, emotional, mental, social, spiritual, and professional well-being, you can create a balanced and fulfilling work-life experience. Remember, self-care is a personal journey, and it is important to find what works best for you. Prioritize your well-being, and you will be better equipped to handle the demands of the workplace and be able to thrive.

However, sometimes you may have struggles and symptoms regardless of self-care, and you may need some people to help. It is okay to ask for help, and it can be easy to do with an effective care team. We'll talk about that in the next chapter.

Chapter 9

Care Team, Assemble!

One of the most effective things I ever did for my mental health was allow the people around me to help me. Once I finally reached out to my loved ones about what I was experiencing, I started receiving support from so many people who I never expected would care about my issues.

As the years have gone by, I've built an incredibly supportive care team. To some, a care team refers to just doctors and nurses. I have expanded the term *care team* to include anyone who assists with someone's journey to stability. I consider my wife, mother, siblings, medical providers, close friends, and even some coworkers as part of my care team. Having a well-established care team has been instrumental in helping me find resources, accommodations, coping mechanisms, and motivation.

The best way to describe my care team is by dividing it into several categories: clinical care, family care, peers, and social group/coworkers.

Here's who is in each category, from the bottom up:

- The base or foundation of my care team is the clinical category. This consists of my doctor, psychiatrist, therapist, and the nurses who all have been a part of my treatment journey over the years.

- The next group is my family. This consists of my wife (caregiver), my mother, my siblings, and my closest friends who all supported me through my mental health aliments but also helped me get early intervention and the help I needed.

- The next group is my peers. This includes people I met through peer support, meaning other mental health advocates and individuals with similar mental health experiences.

- Lastly, the final group is my social group, which includes people I was able to engage with once I was more stable, which includes some of my coworkers and several of my neighbors.

All these people in these different categories have played an important role in my stability, which was possible because of a foundation of clinical care and resources.

This may look different for others if their family played a more important role in getting initial care or if someone doesn't have family or friends to rely on as a part of their care team. However, these groups will be important to anyone seeking help with mental healthcare. In this chapter, I will break down each of the groups, whom each group might consist of, and what role they played in my recovery journey.

Clinical

The foundation of my care team is my clinical care team. My primary care doctor is the first person I list because she is the only person who fully understands my complete history and family history with mental health, schizophrenia, addiction, and physical health issues resulting from these ailments. She was also the one who was able to refer me to my psychiatrist. I have had the same psychiatrist since my original diagnosis, and I am aware that most people are not as lucky as I am to have the same providers for almost a decade.

I've already explained how important it is to focus on self-care and identify triggers, but establishing a care team allowed me to have additional assistance and people to go to when self-care just wasn't enough to get by. Different people have played different roles in my care team, and I knew who I could go to with certain questions or if I needed guidance on a specific topic. My doctors and medical professionals were the first people I considered a part of my care team.

At one point I only considered my primary care doctor, my psychiatrist, my therapist, and the various nurses of these doctors to be on my care team.

In fact, conversations with my psychiatrist are where I first heard the term *care team* and started establishing who was a part of my ongoing care. I eventually started meeting with a therapist, and then I started looking at who composed my care team outside of a clinical setting.

My clinical care team was essential for creating a foundation of stability for me to get access to medication and treatment. My clinical team was also instrumental in giving me the ability to focus more on long-term stability and setting goals. Without my medication and treatment, that would never have been possible. They also help me find and maintain effective coping mechanisms and discuss ways to manage shifts in my mental health.

This group of my care team has expanded over the years, going from just my primary care doctor to including my psychiatrist, therapist, and the various nurses and nurse practitioners that I see frequently with my specialists or in hospital emergency settings. I come to my clinical care team with any questions regarding my diagnosis, medication, and ADA workplace policies that may affect me.

If mental health concerns at work become overwhelming or all-consuming, it is important to consider seeking professional help. Mental health impairments like depression and anxiety may not seem serious to those of us who struggle with them, but they can sometimes be caused by serious undiagnosed mental illness that could require more personalized treatment or even medication. Even if there isn't an underlying mental illness diagnosis, feelings of depression and anxiety can still get severe enough to lead to a diagnosis of generalized anxiety disorder or major depressive episodes. If you feel that your mental health concerns are prolonged or create a feeling of being unsafe, it may be time to consult with your primary care doctor.

Family

My family was the part of my care team that got me to start my mental health journey by preparing resources for me while I was struggling with undiagnosed mental illness. When I reached out to my mom and my wife for help, they already had a doctor I could go to, and that is how I got referred to a psychiatrist to get my official diagnosis and start addressing some of my ongoing mental health concerns and symptoms of mental illness.

At the time of my diagnosis, my wife became a caregiver for me until I was able to get stable. No one understood my mental health needs more than she. Allyson is the only person I consider a part of both my clinical and family care teams. The reason I include her in my medical care team is that she has been, at times, my sole caregiver, and she sometimes even knows more about my mental health needs than I do. My clinical care team tends to deal with more of my mental health crises and severe mental illness symptoms, but my wife is the one who is there 24/7 on-site.

My wife has been a critical part of my care team. As someone who was a caregiver for someone else growing up, I never expected to struggle so much that I would also require a caregiver myself. Allyson helped me manage my medications, encouraged me to open up more about my mental health, and even got me to try therapy for the first time. Any time I had symptoms at jobs or needed to leave work early, she would come pick me up. During some of the hardest parts of my life, Allyson was there to help me through.

Having a supportive spouse played a huge role in my getting early intervention for my mental illness and also in seeking help for my mental health issues that I was having from work years later. Not everyone is lucky enough to have a spouse or supportive family like I had. My wife and my family have been so important in my mental health journey in that I could go to them with any difficulties that I was having with work or my personal life.

My family care team also includes my mother, my siblings, and various close friends. I love having this part of my care team to go to with questions about my life changes and decisions, as they have my best interest at heart. Dealing with mental health issues can be overwhelming, and a care team provides encouragement and motivation, helping me stay committed to my treatment plan and making steady progress. I also believe my family and friends are the group of my care team that are most effective in helping me get through periods of burnout and get out of burnout too.

Peers

The next two groups of my care team are where my model of an effective care team may differ from others. Starting with the peer group, this group consists of my peer support groups, fellow mental health advocates, and my social media connections.

Peer support is where I started my journey with mental health recovery and mental health advocacy. The people

I met in peer support groups helped me realize that I was not alone in my journey through mental illness. Meeting other people who were living happy and successful lives despite struggles with mental health issues or mental health diagnoses gave me hope for future stability.

While hosting the *Unseen & Unheard* podcast, I was able to interview other people with schizophrenia and discuss the importance of feeling less alone and meeting people with similar diagnoses, which can make a person feel less alone.

Other Friends and Coworkers

The last group of my care team is my social group. This is the group that I am only able to engage with once I have reached a point of stability. This group consists of my coworkers, several of my neighbors, and some of my other friends. The main reason I include this group is because of the socialization aspect. My coworkers especially have become very helpful in the past with creating meaningful connections and providing more people in my life who can keep me from self-isolation and burnout.

Your Care Team

Now, *your* care team may look different than mine, and that is okay. Care teams usually consist of only professionals, such as therapists, counselors, and psychiatrists, who provide a broad range of expertise and support. But the idea of forming care teams is just to ensure that all aspects of our mental health are addressed, like socialization, emotional support, and medication management. A care team is important for personalized care because mental health issues are highly individual, and a care team can tailor their approach to meet specific needs.

There was a point in my life when I would not have considered that I needed a care team and definitely not a caregiver. I felt ashamed of the idea that I could not take care of myself like other adults in my life. It took a long time for me to be okay with the idea of relying on other people or needing to ask someone else for help. I think this keeps a lot of people from telling their doctors, loved ones, or coworkers what they are going through.

Care teams can be there when self-care just isn't enough. Even if you make all the right efforts to preserve your own mental health and avoid burnout, you may still struggle with ongoing mental health issues. Realizing that was very frustrating. I even stopped trying to take care of myself. I figured that if I was still going to have declining mental health and fall into burnout that I shouldn't even bother trying.

I did not realize how much it would affect me or how quickly I would fall back into mental health issues. Even while struggling with declining mental health, I thought I would be fine. As frustrated as I was with the idea that I would have these issues, despite taking all the right steps to care for myself and educate myself, I would come to realize that *not* taking these precautions could cause a lot of additional stress in my life.

It would cause me to become more irritable, less productive, and less motivated both at home and at work. I even briefly quit taking my medication without consulting my clinical care team. This led to conflicts with my friends and coworkers and showed me how much of an impact not taking care of myself can have. During this time, many of the people in my care team noticed I was struggling and were able to help talk me through the anger and frustration I was having with this period of not prioritizing my own self-care.

My wife, my psychiatrist, and my coworkers all helped me realize not only the importance of my self-care but why I needed them as a care team. In a time where my own judgment was clouded by my declining mental health, my care team was able to work together to get me stable and help me identify why I felt like I suddenly didn't need or want to take care of myself. My wife encouraged me to start taking more time to engage in my hobbies and physical activities again, while my doctors got me to start my medication again, and my friends and coworkers helped me to stop isolating myself and start socializing again.

My care team was there when I didn't even know that I needed them. It can be so difficult to realize that there are some issues with mental health that will outweigh what you as an individual can control. However, that is why you need someone in your corner that can help you through those periods of negative symptoms. Finding my care team gave me even more freedom to enjoy each day with less worry or concern about my future issues because I knew I would have my care team through any future turmoil.

You will build your care team over time, and it may change along the way. It may start small and stay small or it may grow larger as you start asking for support. I am lucky to have found great caregivers in my life.

My message for anyone trying to assemble a care team is this:

You are not weak for needing help. You are not less of a person. You are not a failure. You are not alone in what you are feeling, and you might be surprised how many people struggle in similar ways. I can tell you from personal experience that allowing people to help takes a lot of pressure off worrying about other people knowing that you are struggling and makes it easier to focus on healing. Having a care team can be vital for effectively managing mental health issues as it provides comprehensive, personalized, and continuous support; advocates for necessary accommodations; and helps reduce feelings of isolation and overwhelm.

Having a care team will allow you to have people that you can go to with any questions, concerns, and life changes. The more you share, the more you will be able to rely on these different groups later in life. I would not be where I am today without the care teams that I formed with doctors, family, friends, and even coworkers.

People just starting on their mental health journeys may not have established care teams right away, especially if they are unaware they need help or do not have a mental illness diagnosis. Many people find out later in life, and some not until they are already adults in the workforce. Finding out that you have a mental illness while in a career can be very complicated, which is something that happens to many adults in mental health crisis.

In the next chapter, we'll meet two mental health advocates who were willing to share their personal experiences of working and living with mental illness diagnoses, and how their struggles with mental health issues affected their lives, future plans, and career goals.

Chapter 10

Sharing Stories and the Realities
of Mental Health at Work

Gabe Howard was fired from his job for opening up about his bipolar disorder diagnosis. Michelle Hammer was either fired or forced to leave 10 different jobs for having schizophrenia and issues with negative and cognitive symptoms. These two mental health advocates took the time to share their stories with me about their experiences of having mental illness diagnoses and experiencing negative mental health in the workplace. Both Gabe and Michelle have unique stories that show how stigma surrounding mental health and mental illness in the workplace can keep passionate and motivated individuals from being able to succeed.

These stories show how some employers are not only avoiding mental health in the workplace but also unwilling to see the impact that not having mental health resources can have on individuals who are struggling. Although most of the previous chapters contained tips and best practices, in this chapter I hope to show that sometimes the reality is not always the idealized version. And if you work in management or HR, you will see how important it is to support employees with mental health ailments.

Meet Gabe

Gabe Howard (he/him) is a bipolar advocate and speaker who became known for his advocacy and honesty about his struggles with bipolar disorder. Gabe has struggled with depression, mania, suicidal ideology, addiction, divorce, and much more, all as a result of his bipolar disorder. Gabe lost his job in the computer IT and networking industry in the mid-1990s just for being honest about his diagnosis with his coworkers and his employer.

"If you had asked me 5 minutes before I was diagnosed, I would have told you of course I don't have mental illness," Gabe told me.

While Gabe was advancing as an IT professional during the same time the Internet was growing in popularity, he started dealing with symptoms of mental illness. He had to call in sick to work to go to a psychiatric hospital, where he received a formal diagnosis of bipolar disorder.

When initially calling his work, he simply told them that he was at the hospital and would be gone for a few weeks. When he returned to work 6 weeks later, his coworkers asked him where he had been. He told them very openly that he was suffering with suicidal ideology and was diagnosed with bipolar disorder.

"It was my earliest form of advocacy; I saw no reason to hide. I didn't think anything of it," Gabe told me during our interview. Gabe explains that because he was a young white man in his 20s who had the luxuries of youth, privilege, and being highly sought after in a competitive field, he didn't think that this diagnosis would change anything.

"When they asked why I wasn't at work, I told them the truth. I should have said, 'I was in the hospital, I'm doing better now,' and moved on. But I didn't realize I was supposed to do that to keep my job."

The backlash was almost immediate. When he returned to work, his coworkers accused him of faking his mental health struggles, and one coworker went as far as telling Gabe that he faked being suicidal so that he could get 6 weeks' paid vacation. Gabe assumed that it was only a few people who thought that but realized over time that most of the people he worked with thought this way. He wasn't worried because he assumed that they were only confrontational because he worked in a competitive industry, and he knew that bipolar disorder was just a condition he couldn't control and that should be treated with care and accommodation. Unfortunately, his employers and coworkers didn't feel the same way.

Things got even worse when Gabe continued to open up about his diagnosis and started requesting reasonable accommodations or needing to take time off for appointments or medication changes. When Gabe requested a reasonable accommodation to move to a desk that wasn't in the center of the room, which was causing him anxiety and distractions, his coworkers said he lied to get a better desk.

He also had medication side effects that made him fall asleep in a meeting, which made him need to take another week off to get a medication adjustment. He went from being happy in a thriving career to struggling to get through each day. While struggling with a new diagnosis and new medications with many side effects, he suddenly also found himself ostracized by the people he once considered close peers and friends. Everyone turned on him during a point in his life where he could have used support more than ever before.

Due to feeling isolated and abandoned by his workplace peers, Gabe decided to go to an outpatient program to try to find some stability and support. But while Gabe was in the outpatient program, his employer called him to let him know that they were starting an investigation into all his time off and insurance claims. They said they didn't think he actually had bipolar disorder and needed to further evaluate his situation. Gabe was more than agreeable to consent to an investigation because he knew that he wasn't lying and that he was diagnosed with bipolar disorder by the doctor at the psychiatric hospital.

The investigation came back that Gabe was lying, and the company lawyer claimed that he didn't really have bipolar disorder. Despite having a formal diagnosis from a doctor, they reviewed his medical records and decided that he was faking the symptoms. The company was able to fire him because although it is illegal to fire someone with mental illness or a disability because of the ADA, which had been passed in 1990 and was fairly new at the time, it was *not* illegal to fire someone for "faking" an illness – which his company said that he was.

Gabe took this issue to a lawyer, who basically told him it wasn't worth taking to court and that he would lose. The lawyer told him that it was unlikely that a jury would side with a high-functioning man who did not *appear* to be disabled or struggling. It was also because Gabe had worked well for so many years that the lawyer thought a jury wouldn't be able to believe that he "suddenly" became mentally ill and unable to work.

Since he couldn't find another lawyer who would take the case at the time, Gabe had to reach an agreement with his former employer where they would allow him to keep his health insurance for a while and he didn't need to pay back anything for the tuition assistance that his company had given him. He had to just take the deal and move on.

After hearing Gabe's story, I was shocked that this major company was able to get away with firing him by simply claiming he was faking his medical condition. Hopefully we've come a long way with companies not being able to get away with things like this anymore, but I'm afraid it may still happen. Gabe's story reminded me why it is not enough to spread awareness about mental health and mental illness; we also need to elect officials and support policies that protect workers with health issues (including mental health).

FMLA and EAPs

I asked Gabe if he ever used any workplace mental health resources like FMLA or EAPs while in this role or any other jobs he had after.

He explains that he did actually have FMLA in the job he was fired from. He needed to take time off for his initial 6 weeks of treatment and outpatient care, and he used his FMLA for these various periods and also for psychiatry and doctor appointments. Part of my frustration in hearing that Gabe had FMLA is that it ultimately did not save his job or keep the company from discriminating against him for his health condition. He says that although it was beneficial that he was able to take the time off during these struggles without dealing with pushback or negativity from his managers, he has mixed feelings about the resource because in the end, they were able to find a way around it.

Gabe said that he was under the impression that the FMLA was there to protect his job during these health absences (which is what it is designed to do), but the company used a legal maneuver to find a structure settlement and compromise. The average person cannot navigate the legal terminology or understanding needed be able to defend themselves in a case like this, and he points out that he was at even more of a disadvantage as a person going through mental illness treatment at the time. I also asked Gabe if he had ever used any EAPs while working, to which he explained that he has used EAPs at every job he has had since his diagnosis.

"The hallmark of EAPs is that you can use it for up to six free visits with a therapist. I always had good experiences with it in that, I got my six free visits. That being said, I have mixed feelings about them. I think they are great for someone with mental health issues, but calling them beneficial for someone with mental illness is a bit disingenuous."

Gabe explains that more long-term support and specialists are needed to properly assist individuals with ongoing and persistent mental illness. Gabe explains that he is a huge fan of EAPs and knows that they can greatly help people who need to address life transitions and situational mental health issues but found them to be limiting in his experience with a lifelong diagnosis like bipolar disorder.

> Gabe shares his lived experiences with bipolar disorder and mental health as a speaker, content creator, and podcast host of *Inside Mental Health Podcast*. Find him at https://psychcentral.com/blog/show.

My hope with sharing the stories of Gabe and other advocates is that anyone reading can see that obstacles to getting accommodations and resources for mental health and mental illness in the workplace are, unfortunately, common. This was the case for both Gabe and me, as well as Michelle Hammer, a schizophrenia and mental health advocate who was also willing to share her experiences in the workplace with me.

Meet Michelle

Michelle Hammer (she/her) is a mental health advocate, LGBTQIA+ rights advocate, and person living with schizophrenia in New York City. Michelle received an incorrect diagnosis of bipolar disorder in college and was later properly diagnosed with schizophrenia. She went to college to pursue a career in graphic design, only to lose 10 different jobs before starting her own business as a fashion designer for a Mental Health Clothing brand, Schizophrenic.NYC.

Michelle's new business was a way for her to continue making art while still spreading awareness about mental health awareness and mental illness. She had hoped for a long career in a corporate graphic design role but couldn't find a company that was willing to accommodate her ongoing struggles with schizophrenia and mental health.

"When I think back, I realize that my cognitive symptoms were a big reason why I was being fired or forced to quit these jobs," Michelle recalled.

Michelle mentions that she had ongoing symptoms, including cognitive symptoms that affected her memory, insight, and ability to do certain tasks. She addresses that she was not able to hold these jobs because she had no accommodations or resources to help her stay employed or grow with the company.

Michelle says that her mental health kept her from being offered opportunities within companies and from being able to advance or grow with any organization. She even recalled an internship before her diagnosis in which she was supposed to work for 3 months and then as part of the internship would be brought on to a permanent graphic design role. After the 90 days, her manager brought her to lunch to discuss why he would not bring her on in a permanent position. He said that he needed to see that she was really trying or able to do the job. He then started telling her about himself and how when he was a young designer, he had some personal struggle that required him to have to be on medication.

Looking back, Michelle realized that this was his way of trying to tell her that he could tell she was struggling with something and should seek professional help and possible medication. He said she need to "fix herself" before she could get a job with him or in the company. In a way, he was trying to be supportive by trying to make her aware of her struggles that he noticed, but instead of hiring her on and giving her access to health insurance or workplace resources, he chose to let her go.

What a wasted opportunity. My hope is that through sharing my story and others, we can spread awareness about mental health and mental illness in the workplace.

Through all the jobs that Michelle has been through, she says one of the most beneficial things that an employer could have done to help her mental health was treat her more like an individual and less like a number. "It was a corporate New York City job; if you couldn't do the work, there were 10 people lined up ready to take it."

This obviously put people with mental health issues or mental illness at a disadvantage; people worry that if they reach out for help, ask for accommodations, or are an inconvenience in anyway, they will likely be replaced. In toxic work environments like that, it is clear why someone may feel uncomfortable reaching out for mental health resources – and also how someone could become so quickly burned out.

Michelle said that these employers didn't care about "excuses." They didn't care that her nighttime medications would make her less productive the next mornings or that she would need additional time to learn something because of her cognitive symptoms. They only cared about productivity and numbers.

In addition to feeling limitations for having mental health issues in the workplace, Michelle says she noticed limitations put on women in the corporate world. "You are treated differently. I felt there was a glass ceiling keeping me from opportunities. These jobs were roughly only 25% women, and no women were in leadership roles."

She goes on to say that she already felt at such a disadvantage that she never felt comfortable even telling her jobs about her schizophrenia diagnosis or other mental health concerns. There was only one job that Michelle disclosed to HR that she had schizophrenia. She only told them because she had missed the date to sign up for health insurance and asked if she could bring in a notice from a doctor to get an exception to get on the insurance as it was critical for her to have access to treatment and medication. They allowed her to bring in a letter to get on insurance, but it ended up leading to more issues once leadership and her coworkers found out that she had some sort of mental health issue.

Michelle had an episode at work one day that made her manager question why Michelle looked like she was talking to someone on the phone even though she wasn't. He did not know that she had schizophrenia, and when he brought this to HR, Michelle had to look at the HR rep and remind her that she had turned in a document that explained her situation and that she didn't feel comfortable expanding on it with this manager.

The HR manager said that the manager needed to ignore it and that she had a medical issue that was documented. Unfortunately, this manager was unprofessional in that they told other coworkers what had happened, and one coworker started constantly bothering Michelle about it; leadership and HR did nothing to stop it. The coworker would ask Michelle,

"So, what's wrong with you?"

"What are you sick with? Is it something I can catch?"

"You said you have ADD, but what else do you have?"

Michelle eventually felt that she had to leave this job due to the constant issue of her health being brought into question and her being questioned about private matters. The biggest mistake made by the employer and HR in this situation is that after she had turned in her documents and information, the company provided Michelle with no additional information. They did not ask her if she would be comfortable telling management or coworkers, they did not provide her with any resources or accommodations, and they didn't provide any corrective actions when her mental health became a topic of conversation with the team.

During her time in 10 different jobs, Michelle was never offered any sort of assistance and did not even know that most workplaces had resources like employee assistance programs, the FMLA, and reasonable accommodations. She would eventually go on to start her own business because she was unable to find any companies and employers that were willing to take her mental health issues into consideration or even make her feel comfortable and safe enough to disclose these issues.

Gabe and Michelle are just two of the many advocates who reached out to share about negative experiences in the workplace. I am only using these two stories to show how situations were handled poorly by companies and HR professionals and what impact that can have on the people who may be struggling with some of the most difficult times in their lives. You may have noticed a lot of similar themes between both of these stories but also in the stories I've told about my own experiences navigating the workplace with mental illness and mental health struggles.

Having heard stories like these from advocates and patients all over the country, I hope that showcasing these stories will help HR professionals, employers, and industry leaders in seeing the need to take additional steps to help address mental health in the workplace, including providing options and alternatives in times of crisis, having resources for employees (and being educated on them), being willing to have uncomfortable but crucial conversations, acknowledging and addressing negative workplace culture, and more! Knowing that individuals

Sharing Stories and the Realities of Mental Health at Work

like me, Gabe, and Michelle are seeing these same toxic workplace themes, in Part 3 of the book, I want to address leadership specifically in what they can do to create a more accepting and accommodating workplace for those struggling with mental health.

Part III

Supporting Employees with Mental Health Issues

Chapter 11

"Leave Your Problems at the Door" and Other Outdated Workplace Anecdotes

Toxic workplace environments exist in every big city and small town across America. They exist in every industry and in all different kinds of companies – whether big or small, private or public. Everyone has probably worked somewhere with a negative workplace culture at some point in their life. Unfortunately, for employees with mental health issues or mental illness, these toxic workplaces and their antiquated ideas can be very stigmatizing.

In this chapter, let's evaluate some common and outdated quips and concepts that you may not even realize are offensive:

"Leave your problems at the door."

I remember the first time I was told to "leave my problems at the door" when I arrived at work, and it would be far from the last time I would hear it. The first time was when I was working in a production factory, and I was asked why I wasn't keeping up with my usual production numbers. I thought my manager was genuinely asking as a way to be kind or understanding. So, I explained that I was struggling with a change in my mental health medications that was causing additional symptoms but also major side effects.

Without a pause or any show of concern or empathy, he responded, "Well, we need to get caught up, so when you come to work, you need to find a way to leave your problems at the door."

To this day, I am just as confused by his response as the day I first heard it. I would go on to have managers tell me this in retail jobs, distribution jobs, office jobs, and even as a team lead. It was like they were saying that I was capable of just separating my experiences of my personal life the moment I stepped through the door but I was simply deciding not to. This to me was not only unrealistic but seemed like a way to avoid having conversations about mental health and well-being. Instead of managers addressing the concerns brought to them by an employee, they just tell them to not think about it while clocked in. This is such an insensitive response and will ultimately result in employees not reaching out for help in the future; managers should be offered training in matters like these.

"We are like a family at this job."

Another concerning workplace saying is "We are like a family at this job." Although the idea of employees being a family may not seem problematic, it is often weaponized as a way to make employees feel guilty for setting boundaries, taking time off, or even trying to address conflict with coworkers.

I have seen this in my own experience, but this is also a workplace saying that is discussed widely among job seekers and younger (Millennial and Gen Z) employees online. Creating the idea that your coworkers are your family makes it seem like if you take time off or if the employer doesn't hire enough staff, it is somehow the fault of the employee, not mismanagement or a lack of planning on the part of the business.

This saying is often used in smaller companies. In my own experience, it was more common in restaurant settings and other industries in companies that had fewer than 100 employees. My concern with workplace sayings like this is they can be used to push employees to burnout. I would always feel bad knowing that if I had to call in sick for any reason (even if it was a valid reason) that someone would have to come in on their day off. I didn't want to inconvenience my coworkers, so I would often come in when I was sick or struggling with my mental health. I understand a business needs to continue to operate, but companies that have this type of environment often see the highest rates of turnover, and then more work falls onto the few employees who decide to stay, causing even more stress and feelings of guilt.

"Here are things that take no effort."

I once walked into a workplace as a workplace mental health speaker and saw a sign in the employee breakroom that said, "Here are things that take no effort: Being on time, giving 100%, having a good attitude, and work ethic."

"Leave Your Problems at the Door"

I have seen this posted online as well in different work-places, and as many commentors pointed out, all of those things take effort. Disingenuous ideas like this not only can be unrealistic but can make neurodivergent people and people with mental health issues feel like they are failing to keep up with unrealistic expectations. Some days may be easier to do all of these things than the very next day for a person who is struggling. Employers should be mindful before posting idealized versions of what equals a job well done in the workplace.

"The customer is always right."

We've all heard "The customer is always right." While working in retail and the service industries, I would hear this constantly. To take it as its good-faith meaning, it means a business should try to please its customer by making things right if there is a disagreement about a product.

However, my issue is when this saying is used in a way to allow customers to say or treat employees in a negative way. In retail I had seen a manager excuse a customer's poor behavior for making a coworker of mine cry after almost an hour of insulting them and belittling them. When the manager came over, he apologized to the customer and reiterated to my coworker that the customer was always right even though the request was against company policy and the manager had to make an exception for them.

This interaction not only showed the employees that we couldn't enforce workplace policies but that we could never question customers – even if they were rude or insulting. My coworker left this job the week after this interaction. Interactions like this were daily occurrences and made coming to work exhausting. Environments like this led to quick burnout and high turnover rates. I understand the importance of making customers have a positive experience to get recurring business, but this should not be done at the expense of a worker's mental health and well-being.

"If it's not broken, why fix it?"

"If it's not broken, why fix it?" I have heard this workplace saying a lot in industries involving manual labor, but workplaces that embrace this idea often apply it to everything. Some of my previous employers would say this about outdated policies, about standard operating procedures (SOPs) that were no longer accurate, and even in reference to a lack of employee benefits and resources.

When leadership has a mindset like this, it can often reflect in the company not being up to date in modern workplace policies, trends, and understanding. A similar workplace saying with the same energy is "That's just the way we've always done things around here." Once again, that leaves no room for growth or willingness to try new things. These employers needs to get with the times ASAP.

"Work-life balance."

The workplace terminology of *work-life balance* always seemed like an unrealistic standard as well. It creates the idea that there is a perfect balance between your work life and personal life. In reality, your need to focus on your work life should be an *addition* to stability and fulfillment in your personal life. There are also times in each person's life when their personal life needs to take priority over work life.

Although I don't personally like the term *work-life balance*, I do use it throughout this book because it is commonly used to discuss mental health at work. My hope is that in the future we can recognize that a healthy balance between your job and life outside of work should be the norm.

"Quiet quitting."

Another term that became a huge controversy online and in certain workplaces in recent years is *quiet quitting*. Quiet quitting is the idea that employees become disengaged and start doing the bare minimum until they eventually leave their jobs. Some companies and CEOs took to social media to call out their work-force or employees for "quiet quitting" and shame the employees into being okay with working more, being overworked, being understaffed, being underappreciated, and providing more output for no or inadequate pay or resources. Wealthy business owners like Kevin O'Leary posted on social media, saying that quiet quitting was a career killer and a cancer to company culture and that he would never hire someone who believes in it. But CEOs and one well-known businessman don't want to acknowledge that employees becoming disengaged is a direct result of toxic workplaces and employers not meeting employee needs.

If an employer refuses to acknowledge employee concerns, pay a livable wage, provide insurance or benefits, provide mental health resources, or offer a work-life balance, then employees are inevitably going to start looking for better jobs. That means they will likely become disengaged as they start planning to leave. This was somehow turned on the workforce instead of it being addressed as a shortcoming of employers and companies and their lack of interest in providing a sustainable future for their employees. Let me be clear: there is no such thing as "quiet quitting"; there are, however, more employees that see a disparity in the work they do and the pay and benefits their company provides.

"If you don't like it, you can find another job."

My least favorite workplace saying, this is the most dismissive and unproductive way to address genuine concerns from your employees. The "believe or leave" attitude shows workers that is it not safe or encouraged to come forward with any concerns they may have. This will prevent workers from reaching out for mental health resources, safety concerns, frustrations in changes within policy, and more. Companies that encourage management to say this are creating a toxic environment where workers won't get answers to legitimate questions about policies or company goals but instead get told to just leave and find a new job.

This saying makes employees feel like they are just a number in the eyes of the company and not hardworking individuals who may have invested years of their lives to the same employer. There is nothing more dismissive than not being willing to discuss or even acknowledge employee concerns, especially about policy changes. I have had several employers take on this mentality, sometimes after layoffs, company restructure, or just as a way to enforce unfavorable policies.

I was working for a company that I really enjoyed, that had a positive and supportive company culture, and that had been fairly helpful with and accommodating to my mental health. Unfortunately, after a financially difficult year, the company decided to restructure, which led to firing the CEO, laying off hundreds of employees, and hiring an interim CEO who only cared about correcting the budget, with no regard to the employees who remained. The company culture completely shifted and went from being open and accommodating to being toxic and dismissive. All questions about policy, security, or changes of the company were met with "If you don't like it, you can leave." So I did, along with many of my coworkers.

It honestly seems like some companies embrace some of these workplace sayings with the impression they may help enforce policies or motivate employees. Different industries will have sayings among the employees and sometimes management that feed into a fear of leadership or HR. But the best way to prevent negative or toxic workplaces is just by creating a positive work environment in which employees are encouraged to ask questions and be engaged with their company and role; we'll talk about that in the next chapter.

Chapter 12

How Employers Can Improve Workplaces

It should be obvious by now that workplaces need to change.

HOW WORKERS' JOBS OFTEN MAKE THEM FEEL

30% STRESSED 26% OVERWHELMED 22% ANXIOUS 18% DISENGAGED

50% LIKE THEY BELONG 40% FULFILLED 36% HAPPY

Source: *SHRM Employee Mental Health in 2024 Research Series.*

My message for employers, HR professionals, and managers is this: *you* can change how mental health is addressed in the workplace. *You* can be the individuals in your industry to create a more accommodating and accepting workplace culture. *You* have the opportunity to create an environment that allows people who may be struggling with mental health to feel safe and secure.

You can rebuild your workplace's culture.

In this chapter, we'll talk about how to do that, but first let's talk about *why*.

Why Retaining Employees Is Important

With unemployment rates continuing to decrease since COVID-19, retaining workers is more important than ever, and younger workers will continue to seek work that accommodates their mental health. Millennials, Gen Z, and younger generations are acknowledging mental health and work-life balance more than ever, and they want to work for companies that reflect these beliefs.

I know that there are many companies seeing the effect of negative mental health and toxic workplace culture on the ability to retain staff and find new employees because I have been asked to speak about mental health in the workplace by corporations all over the country and have had HR professionals express their frustrations about seeing a revolving door of workers. There are obviously many reasons that employees leave a job, but issues with management, toxic culture, and burnout are some common reasons.

HR professionals and many executives know that it is cheaper to try to retain an employee than endure the labor and financial tolls of posting a position, interviewing candidates, and onboarding a new hire. They know that hiring someone is a hefty investment. In fact, according to recent data, replacing an employee can cost between half and two times that employee's annual salary.[1] Investing in mental health resources is just another way to try to reduce turnover, keep talent, and have more engaged employees who are proud to represent a company that will back them up if and when they need additional assistance or accommodations.

Before returning to college to pursue a degree in HR management, I believed what many other people in different industries believed: that HR didn't care about my problems and that they were only there to help the company and fire me if I became too much of an inconvenience. After years of working, going to school, and meeting many HR professionals, I now know that this is not true.

Most individuals who work in HR want the best for their peers and coworkers, and that is often the very reason why they went into that field! But it can be so hard for workers to see this if they have only had negative or disciplinary encounters with the HR team. Even if your

---

[1]https://www.lano.io/blog/the-true-cost-of-employee-turnover

company is at the top of its industry in investing in mental health resources and promoting mental health awareness, remember that new employees coming to your company may have worked in other companies or industries and had negative experiences on the job. They might have come from employers that didn't have mental health resources or did not properly address the need for mental health well-being in the workplace. Having open communication and trust with your employees will prevent toxic or negative workplace culture and will help in preventing workplace turnover.

Promoting Mental Health Awareness in the Workplace

There are simple ways to promote mental health awareness in the workplace while also increasing employee retention, trust, and engagement such as having open communication, keeping people aware of what resources you offer, taking preemptive measures to avoid employee burnout, recognizing employees as individuals and not numbers, providing options in times of crisis, and acknowledging and addressing any negative workplace culture in a timely manner.

"It all starts with the culture of being able to speak openly. We've seen the culture shift in terms of being able to talk about mental health in a different way than what we did a few years back, which in many ways is fantastic," says Julia Anas, chief people officer of Qualtrics.

Effective communication is a way that employees can feel more comfortable at work and able to express concerns with their managers and company leadership. If your leadership team has an "open-door policy" and employees are not using that invitation to bring forward ideas or concerns, it can often be because other employees advised them not to.

Having that open communication with employees will allow the company and leadership to know about issues in their workplace, culture shifts, or issues with managers and shift leaders and give them an overall pulse on how their team is functioning. It will not only give employees with mental health concerns an outlet to reach out for help but can give disabled employees, LGBTQ+, and BIPOC (Black, indigenous, and people of color) employees the confidence to come to leadership about issues about harassment or discrimination without fear of retaliation.

Making Sure LGBTQIA+ and BIPOC Employees Have a Voice

The path to a truly inclusive workplace requires a commitment to acknowledging and addressing the different barriers faced by LGBTQ+ and BIPOC employees. Employers can make a safer and more inclusive workplace by implementing policies, promoting diversity in leadership, and providing additional mental health resources. Recognizing these barriers is the first step toward meaningful change and mental well-being for everyone. However, acknowledging these issues without meaningful efforts to address them is a disservice to LGBTQ+ and BIPOC employees.

I want to make sure that I acknowledge my own privilege in my journey through mental health, mental illness, incarceration, and employment. As a straight, White man I think it is important to make sure that readers are aware that I had all the access I needed for mental healthcare, insurance, getting a diagnosis, and even success finding jobs after being incarcerated. Although I did have many struggles and hardships in my journey, I had access to resources and support that many people in different communities do not have. It is important to discuss how LBGTQIA+ and BIPOC in America may have even more barriers when it comes to obtaining assistance for mental health and facing discrimination in the workplace.

To comprehend the current barriers, it is important to consider the historical context of marginalization that both LGBTQ+ and BIPOC communities have faced. For centuries, these groups have endured systemic discrimination, which has contributed to disparities in health, education, and other opportunities. This historical trauma continues to influence their experiences today, creating a foundation of mistrust and heightened vulnerability in various settings, including the workplace.

I grew up in a small, rural area that had little to no diversity of any kind, and people I knew and worked with could be very closed-minded about people that were different than they. I saw firsthand how employees and even managers would act differently to employees with different backgrounds, beliefs, or cultures. Even in

2024, people still face discrimination in the workplace, which can obviously affect their mental health and well-being. These individuals are at higher risk for a range of mental health issues, including anxiety, depression, and substance abuse. The constant need to navigate a discriminatory environment can lead to chronic stress, which has both immediate and long-term health consequences.

According to NAMI, LGBTQ+ adults are more than twice as likely as heterosexual adults to experience a mental health condition. Transgender individuals are nearly four times as likely as cisgender individuals (people whose gender identity corresponds with their birth sex) to experience a mental health condition. Many people in the LGBTQ+ community will face issues with toxic workplace culture and discrimination due to other workers having different religious and political beliefs.

"They are having a meeting just to talk about the 'gay pride' stuff, trying to force us to be okay with getting gay coworkers." That was a real thing that I heard while working in a production facility that had a single meeting to address how to appropriately acknowledge and understand LGBT individuals in the workplace. I had heard similar comments while working in other industries as well. I reported to HR, with no real resolution in addressing the issues.

In these same workplaces I would see that BIPOC employees would be negatively discussed and face isolation from certain other employees. People of color can experience more barriers in getting employment, having access to insurance, and getting proper diagnoses and treatment. For example, NAMI estimates that Black people are 1.5 times more likely to be uninsured, Hispanic people are 2.5 times more likely be uninsured, and American Indian and Alaskan native people are 2.9 times more likely to be uninsured compared to White people. Historical mistreatment by healthcare systems has fostered a deep mistrust toward healthcare among many LGBTQ+ and BIPOC individuals. The stigma associated with mental health issues can also deter these individuals from seeking the help they need.

Even if BIPOC individuals have access to mental healthcare and insurance, they may still face discrimination from employers by not receiving adequate or equal accommodations. According to the Society for Human Resource Management (SHRM), employees of color with disabilities are less likely than their White counterparts to receive workplace accommodations. This SHRM study also shows that men and women of color with disabilities face more discrimination and harassment in the workplace. Many workplaces lack comprehensive anti-discrimination policies that are put in place to protect LGBTQ+ and BIPOC employees. Without these protections, individuals are more susceptible to discrimination, harassment, and unequal treatment.

The study estimates that about 34% of all people with disabilities reported experiencing discrimination and harassment at work. However, among all employees with disabilities, about 39% of BIPOC women and 41% of BIPOC men experienced harassment and discrimination, compared with 27% of White men and 33% of White women.[2] These statistics show an unfortunate trend in people of color experiencing higher rates of workplace discrimination while already dealing with issues of managing and working with different disabilities.

A common reason that discrimination and harassment can occur is that employers often do not provide sufficient training on issues related to diversity, equity, and inclusion. This lack of education can lead to microaggressions, unconscious bias, and other forms of discrimination that adversely impact the mental health of the individuals in the LGBTQ+ and BIPOC communities – even if other employees don't *intend* to have bias.

Not being able to receive proper mental healthcare, access to insurance, or workplace accommodations make it that much more difficult to be able to succeed and thrive at work while dealing with these barriers both at work and in everyday life. I cannot personally speak to these issues, but I wanted to make sure to at least acknowledge these topics because the recognition of unique challenges faced by BIPOC employees is critical in taking the first step to making changes to workplace culture that allow every employee to succeed and thrive.

---

[2]https://www.shrm.org/topics-tools/news/inclusion-diversity/disability-inclusion-racial-bias

A very important part of rebuilding culture and having open communication can be making sure that *if* employees start reaching out about concerns or issues with coworkers or managers, they are not met with retaliation. Be sure to let employees know that they need to reach out if there is any form of harassment or retaliation from peers or direct supervisors.

In a toxic work environment, certain employees or peers may try to make an employee feel unsafe or guilty for speaking to leadership about issues they are facing. If employers can create a safe and supportive culture, they can have more success in having an open dialogue with their employees. Everyone should work in an environment that they feel comfortable discussing their mental health or issues with coworkers without fear of stigma, occupational setbacks, or repercussions.

On a higher level, there is a lot that people at the top of the company can do that managers and direct supervisors cannot implement. Company owners and executives should ensure that employees have access to training and resources to help them manage their mental health and should implement policies and practices that promote mental well-being, such as flexible working arrangements, reasonable workloads, and support for work-life balance. I know that in companies that I have worked for in the past, HR led a lot of these initiatives, but executives can and should be more involved with these initiatives as well.

In addition, people at the top of the company should be more aware and proactive in identifying and addressing workplace stressors that can negatively impact mental health. This can involve regular assessments of workplace culture, workload, and employee satisfaction. Some companies will use culture surveys for employees to take, but I have seen those surveys not used to implement any change or adjustments based on the employee responses. Why even have them if you don't intent to make adjustments based on how your workforce answers?

Culture surveys are a great way to have an insight you might otherwise not have into how people really feel in your work environment. However, if there are never any changes or even acknowledgments of areas that need improvement, eventually employees will stop taking them seriously and stop providing insight into your workplace.

Employees notice when there is a lack of mental health resources, but according to the 2024 Society for Human Resource Management (SHRM) Mental Health in the Workplace study,[3] so do HR professionals. Only 35% of HR professionals said their organization is effective at supporting employees with mental health concerns. That means almost two-thirds of human resource professionals who were polled aren't seeing an effort on behalf of their employers to support mental health awareness efforts or resources. Although I was disappointed to read this statistic, I was not surprised.

Some employers have claimed to be pioneers in "mental health in the workplace" efforts but have made no real

---

[3]https://www.shrm.org/topics-tools/news/all-things-work/mental-health--hr-and-the-workplace

How Employers Can Improve Workplaces

efforts to implement any meaningful or effective policies to help individuals with mental health concerns. With mental health being a trending topic of importance to employees and job seekers, some companies (and even other mental health advocates) have done a disservice to the mental health movement by using terminology and buzzwords to make it seem like they care about the state of mental health in the workplace.

In recent years there has been "watered-down" and generic mental health in the workplace campaign efforts that sometimes only entail sending out a mass email telling workers about "Mental Health Awareness Month" but don't follow up with resources, education, or genuine efforts to improve the lives of employees living with mental health and mental illness. Some companies try to initiate mental health activities or awareness campaigns with the best of intentions but can fall short if there isn't proper research or education put into these efforts.

An effective way to provide services, policies, and mental health initiatives that actually benefit employees may be to ask employees what *they* think would be the most beneficial. A poll listing choices between having mental health days, wellness fairs, mental health month activities, and workplace mental health trainings will allow employees to feel like they are involved with the decision.

This can be done through culture surveys, or it could also be done separately as its own poll. A benefit of doing this and allowing employee engagement with this effort is that it will make them feel more like the company values their voice and opinion. You may also be shocked to see the results. In some workplaces, the smallest gestures and attempts to improve employee morale can greatly impact employee mental health.

Some employees have had success with implementing less costly investments to mental health, having mental health trainings, activities, and awareness days. I've seen success with a few unique mental health initiatives from a company that I worked at as a custodian. Even though I wasn't in an office role, this company gave access to personal and professional training and resources to every employee. This was a bigger company than I had ever worked for before; they employed office workers, production workers, distribution center workers, and many more.

There were three different mental health initiatives that this company took that made me feel like they actually cared about mental health awareness outside of them just providing resources like EAPs and workplace accommodations for employees:

- **Paid and unpaid trainings for personal and occupational development:** The company had a team in HR that worked on developing and hosting various trainings for different types of personal and professional growth. Some were focused on mental health, self-care, and understanding/preventing workplace burnout. These paid trainings were available to anyone and were offered at various times throughout the year. They were not mandatory, just an option for anyone who was interested. This not only showed that the company cared about making mental health awareness more accessible, but that they also understood that employees cared about these issues.

- **Awareness efforts (not just in May):** As I stated before, it can be frustrating to see Mental Health Awareness used just as a trending topic or "buzzword." I would constantly work at companies that would share a post on May 1 for Mental Health Awareness Month (a nationally designated month) or send a mass email about mental health but then not acknowledge it or speak about it any other time. This company would not only have the general "May Is Mental Health Awareness" email acknowledgments but would follow up with educational content about mental health *and* mental illness. They did a "wellness fair" in May and brought in people from the company's EAP, local peer support group leaders, HR reps with information on *all* of the company's mental health resources, and more! Although there *was* more of a focus on these classes, activities, and resources during Mental Health Awareness Month, what I appreciated was that they would still offer most of these things throughout the rest of the year. Awareness didn't end just because May ended.

- **Education and activities surrounding the pillars of self-care:** Throughout the year, this company also offered different activities and classes about the seven pillars of self-care that I mentioned earlier in the book. They would also have self-care activities that people could attend (during the workday) like team mental health walks, yoga, educational sessions, peer support groups, and more.

I also greatly appreciated that during these events and educational workshops, mental illness education and awareness were not forgotten. Even companies that are excellent about discussing mental health sometimes leave out mental illness because it can be a more difficult and serious topic to discuss. Mental illness diagnoses are much more common than the average person thinks, and keeping it part of general mental health awareness efforts makes a huge difference in changing people's perspectives on disorders like schizophrenia, bipolar disorder, and borderline personality disorder (BPD) and in helping to combat the stigma around these illnesses.

All these initiatives were so effective in showing the company's willingness to invest in employee well-being. They all required various levels of financial and time commitments that the company made so that employees could feel more comfortable talking about and addressing their own mental health, and it worked.

In this office, I heard more positive conversations about mental health, mental illness, and self-care than in any other workplace I have ever been in. By making mental health a common topic of conversation, employees would discuss mental health as it pertained to themselves, people they knew, or even in media. The efforts of this company were truly working to normalize these topics and create a positive work environment for all employees, which was another reason why this company was a coveted place to work in the area. They had lower turnover rates, incredible word of mouth in the community (which was why I applied to work there), and were able to be selective in hiring due to a large candidate pool to choose from.

Mental Health Awareness on a Budget

Not every company has the resources or capital to invest the amount of time and money into employee retention or mental health efforts like the example I just described. There are companies that have to rely on a single HR manager instead of an HR team of 10. So, what are some ways that managers and leadership can start addressing mental health if they are a smaller team or don't have the funding to provide in-house trainings, large wellness events, or certain mental health resources?

I have seen individuals in leadership and HR implement the following four ideas to go above and beyond without having to make huge financial investments. These are all things that management and leadership could do with just a bit of research and time.

- **Compile a list of local and community resources:** It is great if your company has an EAP or any nation-wide mental health resources, but I found that local nonprofits and peer support groups were able to help me more in times of crisis. Just a bit of research will tell you if your area has any local mental health organizations or in-person peer support meetings.

  Then, if you have any employee come to you with mental health concerns, you have even more resources they can look into. Everyone's experience with mental health issues or mental illness is different, which means that people will have different needs through recovery as well. It makes sense to have many different options in case the employee doesn't have success with the company's existing resources. No matter how good your company is with access to resources, it is always a good idea to have local mental health options too.

- **Take trainings and educate yourself:** Being educated about general mental health and mental illness can help a leader be more effective in recommending certain resources. There are also many free trainings online that can help managers and HR gain an insightful understanding to the mental health needs of your employees. Organizations like NAMI (National Alliance on Mental Illness) and SHRM (Society for Human Resource Management) have great information and studies pertaining to mental health and mental illness and the workplace.

- **Start a peer group:** Another way to find options that may be beneficial to your employees could be to start an employee mental health peer group or council that could meet to discuss the current state of the work environment, the needs of the employees, and the possible solutions that may be an option. Having a group like this that can come back to leadership with ideas and concerns can help employers see how much employees care about mental health as a workplace topic but also what issues the employees believe contribute to any mental health concerns.

- **Set your team up for success:** The best way to keep employees from needing mental health resources as frequently is by setting them up for success. This will include many of the themes previously discussed, including creating a positive work environment and having open communication with employees. This could also include preemptive steps like not under-staffing, as that can cause employee burnout, or addressing any concerns of negative or toxic workplaces.

Be Proactive

My final note for employers attempting to rebuild a work-place culture is to be flexible and consider allowing adjustments to help employees *before* there is a legal need for accommodations. US employees believe that other than paid and unpaid time off, workplace adjustments and flexible schedules are the most important accom-modations. An example of workplace adjustments may include the ability to work from home (if possible for the industry or job). An example of flexible schedules would include part-time work or being able to adjust starting/ending times. Not every workplace or industry will be able to accommodate changes like these, but if it is possible for your company to accommodate these requests, it can greatly improve employee morale and attitudes.

Employees in many industries have been pushing to have more resources and accommodations, as well as supportive cultures. Toxic work cultures will make retaining good employees so much more challenging. I hope these tips are useful for leaders who are looking to restructure or improve company culture. All of the tips I've shared in this chapter are based on successes I've seen from my own employment journey or have been shared by employers and employees that I have met while speaking with companies about mental health in the workplace. Next, I will address what leadership can do to support or nurture employee mental health.

Follow Through

Without a stable mental health foundation, I would not be able to focus or perform my job thoroughly. It can be difficult for employers to see how the impact of negative mental health and workplace culture can truly affect them. I've been lucky enough to speak to workplaces all over the country about mental health and mental illness in the workplace, and when I have spoken to executives and human resource professionals, they always want to know about the return on investment of funding workplace mental health resources.

In today's modern workplace, the mental well-being of employees has become a critical factor for organizational success. A lack of mental health resources can lead to high turnover rates, less productivity, and less company engagement. I found that I and many of my peers were jumping from one workplace to another to try to find an employer that understood the importance of providing adequate resources for employees who may be struggling with mental illness or mental health issues.

Conversations about mental health have gained significant traction in recent years online and in the workplace with many workers and advocates. In addition, mental health accommodations and resources have been more sought after by employees since COVID-19. And many employees are experiencing increased mental health issues like stress, anxiety, and burnout. The necessity for businesses to prioritize mental health is more important than ever because mental health is not just a trending topic or a buzzword; it is a main focus to many workers who are seeking a work-life balance.

Another example of how leadership can play a role in mental health in the workplace is how leadership and HR professionals react to an employee disclosing a diagnosis or requesting reasonable accommodations. It is important to remember that when I talk about "playing a role in mental health," I am hoping that leadership chooses to take an active, positive role because every action can affect a mental health at work. However, sometimes the actions of leadership can actually take on a negative role or influence in employee mental health in a negative way. An example is how an employer had a negative effect on my mental health by not honoring my accommodations.

I had a job in which my reasonable accommodation was a change from first shift to second shift while working as a custodian. This allowed me to be in the office after everyone had left, which made me feel less overwhelmed and kept me from struggling with increased anxiety and paranoia.

Although my manager and HR had approved this request, after about 6 months, they decided to claim that it was no longer a reasonable request. I followed up to inquire as to why, and they said that I should be there when the rest of the team was there despite it making more sense to have custodial there after everyone has left and not trying to clean around employees during typical business hours. My manager even said that my performance wasn't an issue, it was just to "improve team morale."

Her suddenly having an issue with my working-hours accommodation quickly led to this manager being more watchful of my everyday tasks and less willing to accommodate any of my needs as someone with a mental health issue. This was incredibly frustrating because until that point I had been very upfront with her and told her more than what I needed to according to ADA laws.

How she reacted and how HR supported her actions made me feel like I was being forced out through policy changes and workarounds. Leadership made a decision to not support me or my accommodations, which played a role in me not being able to continue my employment there. HR and management can choose to have a positive role in mental health, and as leaders you should know that these moments – both the good and the bad – do not go unnoticed by employees.

Setting the Tone

Effective management and leadership are crucial in creating a functional and mental health–focused work environment. Managers, executives, and HR professionals often set the tone for the company culture and can influence the attitudes and behaviors of their employees. Creating an open and supportive culture is fundamental to addressing mental health in the workplace. This involves fostering an environment where employees feel safe to discuss their mental health issues and seek support. Leaders can take several steps to achieve this:

- Openly discuss mental health in meetings, newsletters, and other communications. This helps to normalize the conversation and reduce the stigma associated with mental health issues.

- If they can, leaders should share their own experiences with mental health, where appropriate, to encourage employees to do the same. This helps to remind anyone that they are not alone and that it is normal for anyone to have mental health struggles.

- Ensure that employees have access to safe spaces where they can discuss their mental health concerns confidentially. This can include both employers' provided resources and public resources. A few examples are one-on-one meetings with managers and HR, mental health hotlines (like 988), and EAPs.

This involves openly communicating about mental health issues and encouraging employees to share their experiences and seek help when needed. Employers and managers who prioritize their own mental health and model healthy behaviors set a positive example for their teams. This can include taking regular breaks, managing stress effectively, and seeking support when necessary.

My manager at my most recent job not only reached out to check on my mental health periodically but would frequently open up about his own concerns, stresses, and struggles. This made it much easier for me and other employees to be honest with him and trust him. I knew that when I came to him looking for suggestions or resources, he would either know where to find them or whom he could ask in HR to get me the answers because he had used some of these resources himself. Sharing stories about his own life, past work experiences, and his personal aspirations made it so easy to connect and communicate with him.

Supervisors and managers might be the first people that employees feel comfortable reaching out to because they may be the only "leadership" that they speak to everyday. Some employees might not understand the role of HR and will confide in direct leadership first. I did that in my first attempts to reach out for help, and as I shared, these experiences were not positive. Supervisors, managers, and shift leads that may be reading this should know that because you spend the most time with employees, they might come to you with concerns, and how you react can determine not only whether they reach out for help in the future but how they will view all leadership at the organization.

These are just a few examples of ways that leadership could be more involved in mental health awareness efforts in their own workforce. There are many other options like monthly meetings with team leaders and HR, utilizing employee culture surveys, and more. Perhaps one of the most important things leaders can do is to ensure they are taking care of themselves. Mental health advocates and caregivers always say, "You cannot pour from an empty cup," in reference to making sure we take care of ourselves before we try to care for others. I believe leaders should keep this in mind if and when they decide to become personally invested in improving workplace mental health.

Leading by Example

Motivated leaders in companies may read this book and feel inspired to make changes, implement policies, and start initiatives to promote mental health and mental illness awareness. It can be important for them to remember to take care of themselves too. The conversation with mental health extends to *all* workers on every level. Mental health does not discriminate and can affect CEOs with the same destruction and persistence that it affects any other person in a company.

In fact, most HR professionals said they take pride in their work (95%) and find it meaningful and purposeful (93%), according to SHRM's Employee Mental Health in 2024 Research Series.[4] However, 50% said their jobs had taken a negative toll on their mental health and well-being, while 52% said they wouldn't recommend the field to someone already struggling with mental health issues.

This poll shows how HR professionals, who are often leading the efforts of working with companies to provide and expand employee mental health resources, are struggling

---

[4]https://www.shrm.org/topics-tools/news/all-things-work/mental-health--hr-and-the-workplace

themselves. I know from my conversations with HR professionals that there are several factors contributing to the declining mental health in this field, including:

- Dealing with constant emergency and disciplinary issues
- Lack of support from company leaders
- No support in correcting or addressing toxic workplace culture
- Being passionate about helping employees but being unable to make changes to accommodate or assist employees who may be struggling

I had a conversation with a former HR professional that explained her frustration that her previous employer would opt to try to remove an employee that was struggling with certain issues that may have caused them to be less reliable or more of an inconvenience instead of finding solutions. After speaking to some of these employees, she would find that they often were struggling with mental health issues but were previously and otherwise very reliable employees. The company would usually move forward with termination instead of trying to find resources or other options for these individuals, which caused her a lot of frustration and discomfort and led her to leave the HR profession.

HR jobs and all forms of leadership can be incredibly stressful and complicated at times. There are so many driven, motivated, and passionate people in these roles, and you all as leaders have the opportunity to create the most impact in mental health awareness and policies that can benefit both employees and leadership.

Leaders who prioritize their own mental health and display healthy self-care behaviors can have a significant impact on their employees. By demonstrating that it is possible to balance work and mental health, leaders can inspire their employees to do the same. In my own experience, there are several steps that a few of my managers took to focus on self-care and in doing so made me feel more comfortable at work.

Managers should try to demonstrate effective stress-management techniques they might use themselves to show that they value work-life balance, and help employees see successful ways to manage stress at work. Workplace leaders can also seek support for their own mental health to encourage their employees to do the same and to promote healthy lifestyle behaviors. Doing these things will help employees but are also recommendations that I use to remind managers and executives to utilize these resources and prioritize self-care for themselves too.

The Benefits of Supporting Employees' Mental Health

When managers, HR, and executives are proactive in identifying and addressing stressors in the workplace, conduct regular assessments of workplace culture, have open communication with their employees, provide and promote mental health resources, and address any toxic behaviors and environments immediately, everybody wins. Here are just some of the positive results you may see:

- Reduced stigma associated with mental health issues and employees encouraged to actually seek help when needed. This can lead to early intervention and prevention of more serious long-term issues like burnout.

- Improved employee well-being and productivity. Employees who have access to mental health resources are more likely to be engaged, motivated, and productive. I know from personal experience that it is way easier to be engaged with my work and my company's mission if I don't have to worry about issues associated with mental health or overcoming workplace negativity.

- Reduced absenteeism and turnover. When I had access to mental health resources like EAP, FMLA, and accommodations, I was far less likely to take time off due to mental health issues and more likely to stay with the company. This is true in my discussions with other mental health advocates as well.

- A positive organizational culture. Employees who feel supported and valued are more likely to be satisfied with their jobs and committed to the organization. It is also important to remember that word of mouth can be very powerful, and having a positive workplace culture will lead to a greater selection pool for candidates. This is especially true in smaller towns or rural areas. Everyone in a small town or region knows which companies are best to work for and most accommodating based on experiences from other people they may know, and they will seek to work at those that come highly recommended by friends and family. Companies with negative organizational culture may struggle to find qualified applicants.

At the end of the day, leadership's role in mental health is to create the best possible work environment, which will help retain more employees and provide resources for you and your team. Not every company has a huge budget or endless access to resources, but it is about doing as much as possible given company abilities. Remember that there are resources and mental health options that are online, affordable/free, or even widely available to the public.

Mental health awareness is more than just people knowing about mental health; it is really understanding how it affects everyone and acknowledging that it can affect anyone. Companies, managers, and HR professionals have such control over workplace environments that there is inherent responsibility that comes with that power. Employees often feel like leadership have no idea what happens in the office, in the warehouse, in the factory, or on a remote site. No matter what type of business you are in, mental health conversations are happening. You have an opportunity to join your employees in the conversation and show them that you care about their well-being at the workplace.

Chapter 13

How My Coworkers Made Work Possible for Me

Work can already add additional stress to a person's life, and building relationships within our workplace can sometimes negatively affect our mental health as we do not get to choose our coworkers.

It is so important to recognize how taking time to support our peers through mental health challenges can make it easier for them, especially if they get little to no support in their personal lives. At any given moment, a coworker you know may be silently battling with anxiety, depression, or other mental health issues. It is crucial to create a safe and nurturing environment that promotes mental health awareness, and I am so lucky that I have had coworkers in many different jobs go out of their way to help me during mental health struggles.

The first time a coworker cared about my mental health and could see that I was visibley struggling was while I was working in a distribution center. I was distressed because I had received my schizophrenia diagnosis, and although I was having success with medication and treatment, I was having some side effects to my medications, and I was struggling more with depression than ever before as a result of coming to terms with my diagnosis and understanding that I was going to have to live with mental health ailments for the rest of my life.

My diagnosis felt like a death sentence, and I felt very alone, confused, and scared. At this point I had already had some of the negative experiences I mentioned with HR, management, and even my peers. So, I was far too nervous to open up to anyone about my diagnosis.

The coworker who I opened up to was able to listen attentively, show empathy to my situation, and offer advice that would forever change my outlook on mental health at work and also how I approached it with my employers.

"I have never told this to anyone here except for HR, but I have major depressive disorder," said my coworker quietly so that no one would accidently overhear.

"It caused me to miss a lot of work, and I almost lost this job. My doctor told me to tell HR here. I didn't want to, but I felt backed into a corner, so I did," he continued. "Not only was I able to stay here, but now I am doing much better and have more job security. You do what you want, but I've been there, and I think you should tell them."

This conversation was the catalyst that led to the first story of me telling my HR manager about my schizophrenia diagnosis in Chapter 1. I was only able to feel comfortable enough to disclose my situation because of this coworker, who was willing to share their own experience in addressing their own mental health struggles and being vulnerable and honest with me. This is a perfect example of why peer support groups and having peers you can confide in can be a way for people to feel less alone.

This interaction with my coworker led to me being more open and honest with all of my employers moving forward and even select coworkers as well. In my last job before pursuing speaking and mental health advocacy, I became close enough with several of my coworkers that I would even consider them friends – a first for me. I told all of them about my diagnosis, about my past consisting of addiction and incarceration, and about my social media advocacy efforts. I wanted to be completely honest because I was so tired of masking (see Chapter 6) at my other jobs and trying to act like I did not have any issues just to impress the people around me in hopes of occupational advancement.

I just wanted to be able to be myself and not hide my past or my struggles. These coworkers allowed me to be my genuine self, which made me feel more comfortable at work each day. I became close enough with some of these coworkers that they even started being a part of my "care team" (see Chapter 9) and were essential in helping me in times of breakthrough symptoms (symptoms of mental illness that occur despite success with medication and treatment) and mental health issues. They made sure I was safe at work and supported and encouraged my goals with advocacy outside of work as well.

With my coworkers being accepting of me, I was able to actually focus on thriving at work, reaching new occupational goals and being able to feel like a contributing member of a team for the first time since my diagnosis. I was once struggling with feelings of anxiety and depression, and one of my coworkers could tell that I needed to talk to someone and asked if I wanted to share what I was going through. It was just a small gesture that meant the world to me at the time.

Being a supportive coworker doesn't have to be huge tasks or anything unreasonable. It can just be about taking a moment to acknowledge how they are feeling or empathize with a situation that they might be going through.

As an ongoing issue with my schizophrenia, I would occasionally have breakthrough symptoms at work. In my last job, my coworkers were not only supportive of my symptoms but got to a point where they could tell that I was having symptoms before I even knew. While working there, I had a coworker named Emerson, and the day I first told him about my schizophrenia diagnosis, he did something that none of my coworkers had ever done before: he asked me questions about how he could better help me.

I had only disclosed my mental illness diagnosis with limited coworkers in the previous jobs I had prior. I would always have some coworkers who would be uncomfortable after discovering I had a diagnosis, that they would not respond or would stop engaging with me entirely. I did have a lot of coworkers that were supportive after finding out. But Emerson was the first coworker who I told that followed up with questions about my diagnosis, my mental health, how to best help me while I'm having symptoms, what coping mechanisms I used, and much more. I was grateful, and the effort to learn more about me and my condition was something I never thought a coworker would take the time to do.

By asking these questions, he was able to start being very effective in helping me while I was experiencing symptoms of my schizophrenia. When I started having symptoms, I would have physical movements involved with my symptoms that I would not be able to recognize during those moments. Emerson would see these signs and knew to try to talk to me, try to bring my attention to it, or to let my direct manager know so that he could help me address it or make sure that I had a ride home.

Having a coworker go above and beyond like that made such a difference in my day-to-day confidence and socialization at work. Emerson went so far as to always check on me if I had to call in or leave early due to my mental health and even took time to stick up for me in negative workplace conversations and try to educate or inform people about my issues instead of letting misconceptions and gossip get out of hand. All of these things he was doing to help me were appreciated but were in no way required or necessary. He did them because he was a good guy and considered me his friend.

My last job was filled with supportive coworkers who either supported me by being kind and accepting or by going the extra mile to address any negative symptoms I had.

I have been able to help some of my peers in the workplace too. Because of my open honesty about mental health and past struggles, coworkers would come to me with questions about their own mental health, how to reach out for help, and what resources they should inquire about with our employers. I had a situation in which I assisted a coworker of mine in being comfortable enough to disclose a mental health issue to our employer, learn about and utilize the company EAP, and be able to get the help he needed to thrive at work.

That is what employees can do as peers to go above and beyond. There will always be workplace environments and employees that choose to be negative toward individuals who are different. By going out of your way to be supportive and helpful, you might not realize how much easier you are making it for that individual to come in each day. This employee made each day more possible for me to not only get through the day but to be able to thrive and focus on my occupational growth!

By cultivating a culture of empathy, understanding, and support within our workplace, we can create a safe and inclusive environment where individuals feel comfortable seeking help for their mental health issues. Together, we can make a positive impact on the mental well-being of our coworkers and pave the way for a healthier, happier, and more supportive workplace.

Chapter 14

From Surviving to Thriving
Stories of Success

"We are barely past the starting line, but I do feel like there is a race happening, at least. The change is so marginal from where we were 20 years ago that is almost nonexistent, but it is happening." —Gabe Howard

Gabe's Success Story

Gabe, whom I interviewed in Chapter 10 about being fired for having bipolar disorder, recognizes that there have been improvements in addressing mental health and mental illness in the workplace but doesn't want us to get overly comfortable with where the mental health in the workplace movement is because we still have so far to go. Fortunately, after his horrible experience of being fired in the 1990s, Gabe did go on to have some positive workplace experiences.

He had been through a lot of jobs after being fired that he had to leave because he wasn't stable enough, didn't feel ready, or was pushing himself too much into burnout. So although he had several jobs after being fired, he wasn't able to hold any of them very long. Then he got a job at a smaller company, working again in a corporate IT job.

After his previous experience, he figured that his best bet was to disclose his ongoing mental health issues and bipolar diagnosis to his new employer. After he was able to get through a 90-day probationary period and was officially hired on, he went to HR but did not disclose his diagnosis to his manager or coworkers.

He told his HR team that he had a mental illness diagnosis and ongoing mental health ailments. He told them that he just wanted this documented, and although he didn't need any accommodations or resources immediately, he might in the future. After his past negative experience, he was incredibly thorough. He requested to have it on file and asked to fill out any needed paperwork while he was well so he didn't need to do it when he was struggling or in psychosis.

Gabe said that experience was great. They documented everything. They made him feel heard and accommodated, and they made sure that if he ever needed to take time off or had absences that he could turn them in directly to HR instead of having to explain his situation to his manager or have to disclose more than he was comfortable with.

Gabe said they also did a great job at communicating what he should expect when using his PTO or unpaid time, what reasonable accommodations were, what accommodations may not be reasonable for the type of work he did, and any other information pertaining to the companies' mental health resources.

"I want to make it clear that I never had a mental health crisis while in this job, so I don't know how they would have handled it if I was in crisis," Gabe explained.

"I believe the reason I didn't have a crisis while working here was because I really felt supported, accommodated, and all of that stress was removed from me," Gabe explains.

Having these resources in place and having the support of his employer made his work experience much easier and was likely the reason for his stability while at this job. He says that he considers the actions of this company to be the "gold standard" for mental health and mental illness accommodation.

It was not only that they were so understanding and willing to work with him on any mental health needs but also that when he walked in and said, "My name is Gabe Howard, and I have bipolar disorder," his employer knew exactly what to do. It made him feel like they had helped others with similar issues before and that they understood mental health and had systems in place to properly address his concerns.

Gabe also compared this to working in other companies and industries that would be confused or uneducated about what they should do if an employee came to them with similar concerns. He quotes other employers asking him things like, "Do we need to document this?" or "What is mental illness?," which did not make him feel confident or secure while working at those jobs. Questions like this showed inexperience or unfamiliarity with mental health and the resources that the company may or may not have to assist a person who is struggling.

Gabe also had wonderful experiences working in peer support. After leaving the corporate world, he started working in peer support and began pursuing mental health advocacy. He said he didn't necessarily consider this a positive "workforce" experience because everyone he worked with was a peer who had lived experiences with mental health or mental illness.

I want to highlight peer support as an alternative to those with mental health issues who want to be more involved with advocacy and have not had any luck with traditional careers. There are peer support–type positions becoming more common across the country that may be a realistic option for those already considering a career change.

Michelle's Success Story

Although Michelle did not find success in corporate America, she was able to find success as a self-employed fashion designer! After facing ongoing struggles to maintain employment due to her schizophrenia, Michelle was able to use her graphic design experience and artistic ability to make her clothing brand. Schizophrenic.NYC was the company that came from the ashes of her experiences working as a corporate graphic designer.

Not only does her company provide her income, but it works to simultaneously spread awareness to mental health and schizophrenia awareness. She creates art prints, shirts, leggings, and even pill containers with her artwork. She can be found spending her days doing popup shops all over New York City, creating amazing art and having conversations with people who want to learn more about her diagnosis.

In addition to Michelle's mental health fashion business, she has built successful social media platforms and a motivational-speaking business. Michelle shares her story now through content, speaking engagements, and artwork.

My Success Story

In addition to Gabe's story of a positive workplace and peer support, I wanted to share my personal positive experience with my last job that I had before pursuing speaking, advocacy, and content creation full-time. My last job that I had was a sales job that I was able to work at for more than 3 years, which is the longest I have been able to hold a job since my schizophrenia diagnosis and earliest struggles with mental health. I want to share how I was set up for success by my managers, how HR made sure that I had the necessary accommodations and resources, how my co-workers helped me in times of crisis, and how all those things gave me the stability to pursue advocacy full-time.

This job was the first job that I got after losing my previous job during the COVID-19 lockdown. I was actually doing very well before COVID-19. I was the most stable I had ever been in my mental health journey; my new medication was working well and had minimal side effects, and I had returned to college to study HR management with hopes of helping people with mental health issues and criminal records find jobs. I was also just starting my online advocacy and was using social media to educate people about mental health and schizophrenia to help break down stigmas and misconceptions, but like many others, when the world stopped for the pandemic, so did my life and all my progress.

The pandemic affected most aspects of my life. I started having a lot of struggles with my mental health again and an increase in my schizophrenia symptoms too. I also had to take a break on my education journey, but I continued making mental health content on social media, and there was suddenly a huge influx of people on social media seeking mental health content for the first time. My pages grew quickly, and I reached more than a million followers across social media platforms. I was so grateful for the ability to reach so many people and share my story. However, when the world opened back up, I had bills to pay and needed to get back to work.

When I was originally hired for this job, it was as a customer service employee. I had worked mostly labor jobs and was in need of more office experience if I was going to continue pursuing an education and career in HR. So, I took this job and was able to use my knowledge of mental health, HR education, and my lived experiences to set myself up for success with this employer, and it ended up being an amazing workplace experience.

As soon as I was hired, I told HR about my schizophrenia diagnosis, my reoccurring mental health concerns, and my possible need for future reasonable accommodations, and I even took it upon myself to learn all about the company's mental health resources like their EAP, FMLA, and company-specific resources.

Although I didn't utilize any of these resources right away, there was a comfortability and feeling of safety in knowing that they were there. After I had been employed with this company for only a few weeks, I made the decision to start an open dialogue with my hiring manager and our store manager about everything I had disclosed to HR.

Although it is not always necessary to tell management and may in some workplaces be counterproductive, I took the chance, and I was met with compassion, empathy, and understanding from both of my managers. They did not judge me; they did not change the way they spoke to me or treated me. This continued to make me feel more secure in my role and with the company, and over the next 6 months, I would have periodic issues with mental health but was able to have them resolved and addressed quickly thanks to the open communication I had with HR and my managers and the care teams I had put in place.

After 6 months in customer service, I made a transition to sales because I just wanted to try something new and challenge myself. I didn't expect to enjoy the new job as much as I did, and I even started to become close friends with some of my coworkers. Then I decided to do something I had never done before at a job: I started having open conversations with all of my coworkers about my schizophrenia diagnosis, my mental health journey, and my past of addiction. For the first time in my entire employment career, I had support from HR, management, and my coworkers.

I cannot explain how freeing it was to be able to be myself, not mask, and talk openly about my mental health. Although I would eventually experience periods of mental health struggles and worsened mental illness symptoms while at this job, it was minimal compared to my previous jobs, and I never found myself in burnout while employed there. When I *did* have symptoms or mental health concerns, I was able to utilize the company's employee assistance program and FMLA.

My managers and coworkers came to know me and my symptoms so well that they were often able to tell that I was struggling before I was even aware, which allowed me to recognize my symptoms and start addressing them immediately. As I had shared in the chapter about my coworkers making work possible for me, their willingness to not only listen to me discuss mental health or schizophrenia but to ask questions if they didn't under-stand showed me how much they cared about making me feel welcome and accepted at work. One of my favorite stories from this workplace is a situation that showed how effective it is to have a plan in place in case of crisis and also how much my managers cared about me and my well-being. This story is about one of the times that I had breakthrough schizophrenia symptoms while at work, and they went above and beyond to make sure I was safe. As I had mentioned, even with medication and treatment, I will occasionally still experience breakthrough schizophrenia symptoms like visual and auditory hallucinations. My coworkers had had encounters with me like this before and knew what to look out for.

One of my coworkers noticed me showing signs that I was having hallucinations and immediately notified my manager. My managers immediately came up to check on me and pulled me aside, away from customers and coworkers, so I wouldn't be embarrassed. The store manager let one of my coworkers know so they could take over any clients I had that needed to be attended to.

At the time of this situation, I lived an hour away from my job and was commuting each day. My manager knew that the first part of my symptom/crisis plan was to contact my wife so she knew that I was having symptoms and that my managers had made sure I was in a safe place. Schizophrenia symptoms can be a bit unpredictable and can devolve quickly. My manager knew that I stayed at the hotel down the block when I was having symptoms since I would not be able to drive home.

They drove me to the hotel and then texted me to make sure that I was safe and checked in. One of my coworkers also followed up just to make sure I was doing all right and didn't need anything. A few hours later, when I ordered food and had it accidentally delivered to my workplace, my manager went out of his way to bring it to me at my hotel and check in on how I was doing.

I am grateful that they were always so responsive when I had symptoms like this. It meant so much to me because I know that employment law and disability law didn't require them to do any of the things they did for me that day – or any other day I had symptoms. Aside from not discriminating against me for my symptoms, everything else they did was out of compassion and empathy.

My manager could also tell when I was dealing with mental health issues like anxiety or depression and always reached out to me to check on me and see how I was doing. These brief moments of support made such a big difference in helping me be more engaged and productive at work while also preventing me from falling into burnout. Over the years of me working there, having all this support made it possible for me to get to a point of stability that I never thought would be possible for someone with constant mental health issues and a schizophrenia diagnosis. It was because of this stability that I was able to focus on my long-term personal and professional goals that led to my career in speaking and advocacy.

This last venture with my employment journey showed me the difference that having a supportive manager, open communication with coworkers, and a positive work environment makes for someone struggling with mental health.

Having all these positive things at work resulted in several aspects of improved mental health and daily work life:

- Needing to take off less time for crisis care and in-patient psychiatric visits
- Having the ability to focus, learn, engage, and thrive in the workplace
- Increase in productivity, efficiency, and ability to perform at a high level
- Less tendencies to self-isolate, leading to an ability to be more social and create more meaningful relationships both at work and at home
- More time to focus on preventative self-care and hobbies

Moving On

Leaving this job was the first time that I had been hesitant to leave a job because I was in a place of stability and mental well-being that allowed me to feel comfortable and supported. I didn't want to leave a safe workplace. All my previous jobs had ended in either severe burnout, declining mental health, or being fired for acknowledging my diagnosis in a toxic work environment. This place was unique in that I genuinely enjoyed the people, the work, and even the leadership. If it had not been for the opportunity to be a full-time speaker and advocate, I am confident I would still be working there.

There are so many stories that I have heard from other advocates in which they have found jobs or careers that have allowed them to stay employed and thrive in the workplace instead of just struggling to get by or working in constant burnout. Mental health support has given so many people the ability to have a career but not at the cost of their well-being. As I said in the beginning of the book, I wanted to work. But for a long time, I didn't think that would ever be possible. Having mental illness or mental health ailments shouldn't remove the option of success or employment.

I am always excited to learn about workplaces in the United States that are going above and beyond to make workplaces more mental health friendly. As I have been asked to speak to workplaces and leadership teams all over the country, I have seen that more people are willing to leave a job to find something that better fits their personal mental health need. I worked in a variety of industries before finding a supportive and positive work environment.

Everyone needs to work to be able to pay bills and support their families, but why shouldn't work be a place that employees can look forward to coming to each day too? Employees want to work for a company that they support and where they align with the mission and company purpose. Unfortunately, I have worked at companies where I aligned with their mission, but they caused me turmoil in my mental health. I left a job that I felt passionate about to take a pay cut because I felt ousted and isolated for discussing mental health and mental illness.

One of the disappointing realizations when writing this chapter about success stories was that it was difficult to find people with such stories to share. Most people who reached out have had more negative experiences or are still trying to find a company mission that aligns with their personal beliefs, an industry that allows them to be themselves without fear of judgment or retaliation, or an employer that simply shows an effort in supporting the wellness and mental health of their workers.

Every day companies are joining the mental health movement, and employees are finding jobs they can feel confident showing up to. There are also new resources, mental health studies, and awareness efforts that are changing what we know about mental health and what options are available for those who are currently struggling. Seeing all the changes is inspiring but also makes me wonder, what does the future hold for mental health in the workplace?

Chapter 15

Redefining Success in the Professional World

When I was first diagnosed with schizophrenia, I was told I would never be able to work. I watched that be true with my mom in her mental health journey, and had it not been for my care team, my success with medication and treatment, and the employers and coworkers who were willing to accommodate my mental health struggles, it is likely that it would have been true for me too.

Unfortunately, many people will never have access to the insurance, medication, and assistance that I had and will likely not even have the option to work. But for the people who can work or are trying to work despite ongoing invisible disabilities, we need to make it possible for them to do so. And we need to make it possible for them to *thrive* in the workplace.

Mental health is in the workplace. *Every* workplace. No matter what business, industry, or company. It always has been, and it always will be.

Not talking about it hasn't worked.

Ignoring it hasn't worked.

Mental health is not going away, so it is time to start addressing it, acknowledging it, accommodating it, and spreading awareness about it. This will allow more people to thrive at work and prevent mass burnout. It will also allow employers to improve retention rates, hire more people, and continue to grow.

No matter your political views or personal beliefs on mental health, it should be agreeable that having a workplace that allows more people to be able to work is a positive thing. Everyone deserves to be able to work, but recovery looks different for everyone. Expecting everyone to fit into the same "box" is not only unrealistic but keeps people from finding success in a workplace. Allowing and implementing the accommodations and resources that I discussed throughout the book is a way to make sure people like me are not forgotten or discriminated against in any industry or job.

People of all generations are beginning to discuss and acknowledge mental health and mental illness in a way that we have never seen previously, especially since the COVID-19 pandemic. Workers are seeking employers that believe in supporting them and their peers, and they are starting to make decisions about their careers based on work-life balance, ability to focus on self-care and family, and what they hear about employers through the experiences of other employees. Companies that are not willing to accept or acknowledge this mental health–focused shift in the workplace will see turnover increase and employee productivity and engagement decrease.

It has been so reassuring that companies, HR professionals, and industry leaders have been reaching out to have me come share my stories about mental health in the workplace, especially because these conversations are not easy. Ignoring mental health and the needs of individuals is an easier option. My hope – in fact, my challenge – for the future of the workplace is that employers choose the option that is less "easy" and take the time and put in the work to help fight mental health stigma and make the American workplace more accessible and accommodating for everyone.

Leaders can normalize mental health conversations in the workplace. They can do what my manager did or what Gabe's HR team did and choose to be accommodating and make us feel less isolated and alone while we are just trying to work like everyone else. Or they can choose to be like the employers that kept people like Michelle, Gabe, and me from being able to get the basic mental health resources and assistance necessary to thrive and succeed at work.

Here's what I hope to see for the future of employment law and mental health in the workplace:

- Additional employment laws to protect disabled BIPOC and LGBTQ+ individuals from harassment and discrimination
- More diverse and unique mental health resources besides EAPs
- Mental health and mental illness awareness trainings for managers, HR professionals, and leadership

- A mental health resource pamphlet provided to every new employee that contains both company and local mental health resources
- More overall employment laws to protect workers for mental health and mental illness–related disabilities

These are just the beginning of what I hope to see in workplaces moving forward. Some of these mental health workplace aspirations could be made possible with the support of company leaders across industries, while others will need the support of advocates and policymakers. All these points could be made possible with the right individuals making mental health in the workplace an industry standard and fighting for more progressive employment laws. Part of making the necessary changes needed for the future of mental health is acknowledging the work that has already been done.

I do think something needs to be said for how far we've come in mental health access in care, even in my lifetime. Although the ADA was signed in 1990, the Mental Health Parity Act wasn't signed for 6 more years. This act made a requirement that health insurance plans needed to provide more equal coverage for mental health and substance use services. These acts have worked to continue to provide protection and prevent discrimination for disabled workers and people all over the country but still have their own flaws.

Although some companies have been providing EAPs and other mental health services, it has only been in the last

5 years that I've seen workplaces really start to provide workplace mental health resources that can make a difference for people like me. This means going the extra mile and truly caring about employees and their lives – even after they clock out. HR and direct supervisors that most commonly interact with employees have the ability to show employees they care by having open communications about mental health at work.

One of the most encouraging developments I have seen is the normalization of mental health discussions. Employees at all levels are increasingly open about their struggles and successes, which creates a culture of empathy and support. This normalization of mental health needs to move past employees and into management, HR, and the offices of company leaders. There is so much power in storytelling. I was shocked to find this as I started my advocacy, but by sharing our stories we can change perspectives on mental health and mental illness in the workplace. You don't need to be an advocate, speaker, or content creator to start talking to your friends, family, and coworkers about mental health. You will see how quickly the perspective and attitude about mental health will change in your circles and your communities if you can have open and honest conversations about it. Storytelling and advocacy are how we can start making these changes for the future.

The future also provides hope for more personalized and accessible mental health resources. Advances in technology have already begun to revolutionize how mental health services are delivered. I have found success in online peer support, social media mental health advocacy, and online platforms. Online platforms can also offer a range of trainings, teletherapy, mental health apps, and peer support apps and can provide employees with flexible and convenient options to support their well-being and reach more underserved communities. There may also be advancements in AI in helping to identify early signs of mental health issues and create crisis interventions. The possibilities are endless.

Again, leadership in fostering a mentally healthy workplace cannot be overstated. My HR manager that helped me get resources, the coworker that shared about his own struggles, and the coworkers who went out of their way to make me feel accepted and "normal" all made it possible for me to even be able to work. I am hopeful as a former HR student that the leaders of tomorrow are being trained to prioritize mental health not just as a checkbox in corporate paperwork but as a core aspect of employee well-being and care. I hope that any leaders reading this, or students with plans to be leaders, understand their role and part in workplace mental health.

An important factor in the future of mental health at work that I have yet to mention is the role of collaboration and community. Businesses, mental health professionals, policymakers, employees, patients, and advocacy groups are needed to join forces to create systemic change or any change at all. I am an independent advocate and speaker, but I work a lot with major employers, local politicians, pharmaceutical companies, and on the boards for several mental health nonprofits. I am fortunate to be able to connect with many people through my social media presence, but real change requires more than just awareness; it requires effective storytelling to help the people writing our laws to better understand the needs of workers, patients, and individuals with mental illness and mental health issues.

Another positive change I've seen since COVID-19 is a growing recognition of the importance of work-life balance and its impact on mental health. Flexible working arrangements, such as remote work and flexible hours, are becoming more common, allowing employees to better manage their personal and professional lives. Many advocates I know have touted the success of these changes and how they have improved their ability to hold and thrive at a job. My wife is an autism advocate that experienced burnout, and she now works from home. For the first time in her working life, she is finally getting resources and accommodations that have made it possible for her to not have to constantly find new jobs or employers.

Finally, the future of mental health in the workplace is largely moving in the right direction because of the numerous mental health advocates, disability advocates, and policymakers who came before me. People who have been fighting for these changes for decades are just now seeing the positive change their work has had. Their courage and resilience have paved the way for a new generation that views mental health with compassion and urgency. Many have been fighting for these changes and policies since mental health was a more taboo and unspoken topic.

I would not be able to discuss these topics and my hope for the future of mental health without the stories of individuals who have navigated their mental health journeys and inspired me (and many others) to continue striving for a world where mental health is prioritized and supported in every workplace – a world where anyone who is able and willing to work has the opportunity to do so. We need to work as hard as the advocates, nonprofits, and peers that prepared the way for us.

There will be so many struggles and setbacks in the future of mental health in the workplace, but there are also so many opportunities for individuals with mental health and mental illness diagnoses. It is important to not glorify the current state of mental health in the workplace or the accomplishments we've made, as we have so far to go. With continued commitment, advocacy, and compassion, we can create workplaces that not only recognize the importance of mental health but actively nurture it. Together, we can build a future where every employee feels safe, supported, and empowered to thrive both personally and professionally. The future of mental health in the workplace will be in remembering the importance of minds over meetings.

Resources

In this appendix, I've provided some links so you can find more information about some of the topics mentioned in this book.

Laws

Americans with Disabilities Act

The Americans with Disabilities Act (ADA) protects people with disabilities from discrimination. It includes a section about mental health and mental illness. See www.ada.gov.

Family and Medical Leave Act

The Family and Medical Leave Act (FMLA) entitles eligible employees of covered employers to take unpaid, job-protected leave for specified family and medical reasons with a continuation of group health insurance coverage under the same terms and conditions as if the employee had not taken leave. See https://www.dol .gov/agencies/whd/fmla.

Legal-Related Resources

Free Legal Support

Know your legal rights as an individual with a disability before you need a lawyer! This government site talks about whether you are covered and what reasonable

accommodations are. See https://www.eeoc.gov/
laws/guidance/your-employment-rights-individual-
disability.

Support Groups

Peer Support

There are several websites where you can find online
peer support groups; these are some options:

Online Support Groups: https://www.psychology
today.com/us/groups

In-Person Peer Support: https://www.nami.org/
Support-Education/Support-Groups/NAMI-
Connection

In-Person Family Support: https://www.nami.org/
support-education/support-groups/#nami-family-
support-group

Career Counseling

Some states have Individual Placement and Support
(IPS), which can help individuals with disabilities find
jobs. For example, in Wisconsin, we have IPS through
the Department of Health Services. See https://www
.dhs.wisconsin.gov/ips/index.htm as an example.

Job Boards for People with Mental Illness

Anxiety and Depression Association of America

This association has a career center to help those
with anxiety disorders and depression find jobs. See
https://adaa.org/jobs-careers-center.

National Alliance on Mental Illness Job Links/Resources

The National Alliance on Mental Illness (NAMI) has a helpful article about this topic. See https://helplinefaqs.nami.org/article/115-where-can-i-get-help-finding-a-job.

AbilityJobs for Disability Talent

The site can match people with disabilities with jobs that might be right for them. See www.abilityjobs.com.

Podcasts

Find these podcasts on your favorite podcast app.

Unseen & Unheard Podcast

To learn more about schizophrenia and mental health, you can listen in to hear me interviewing other individuals living with schizophrenia.

A Bipolar, a Schizophrenic, and a Podcast

Listen to real conversations about living with mental illness from hosts Gabe Howard and Michelle Hammer.

Inside Mental Health Podcast

Inside Mental Health is an award-winning weekly podcast that approaches psychology and mental health in an accessible way.

Acknowledgments

I want to acknowledge my wife for helping me get the stability I needed to be able return to work after my diagnosis. I also want to thank the human resources professionals, managers, and coworkers who went out of their way to help me better understand my struggles and how to thrive in the workplace.

About the Author

Kody Green (he/him) is an individual living with a diagnosis of undifferentiated schizophrenia. Kody is a motivational speaker and content creator with more than 1.5 million followers across social media platforms. He has struggled in the past with drug addiction, incarceration, and serious mental health issues.

To be a better advocate and speaker, Kody has been trained as a peer support specialist, recovery coach, and suicide prevention specialist.

Now, Kody shares his stories about his struggles and how to navigate through recovery, mental health issues, and life after incarceration. He chooses to pursue motivational speaking and mental health advocacy for schizophrenia awareness, drug recovery, and second-chance opportunities because he has dealt with these struggles in his own life. *Minds Over Meetings* is his first book.

Index

Insurance coverage:
  among BIPOC
    individuals, 152
  discrimination in access
    to, 153
  mental health care
    included in, 53
  and Mental Health Parity
    Act, 196
Intervention, early, 20–22
IPS (Individual Placement
    and Support), 202

J
Jobs:
  difficulty maintaining,
    4–6
  evaluating suitability of,
    91–92
  frequent changes in, 80
  maintaining long term,
    8–9
  moving on from, 189
Job boards, 202–203
Job interviews, 39–41
Journaling, 98

L
Leadership:
  making mental health a
    priority, 154–155, 198

mental health
  conversations
    normalized by, 195
mental health of, 168–170
reactions of, to
  disclosures of mental
  health diagnoses,
  164
setting the tone,
  165–168
Learning, continuous, 99
"Leave your problems at
    the door," 135–136
Legal support, 201–202
LGBTQIA+ individuals,
    149–153
Long-term goals,
    evaluating, 91–92

M
Management:
  accommodations
    available through,
    56–57
  informing, of mental
    health struggles, 45,
    49–50, 185
  lack of training in HR
    matters for, 46
  lack of training related to
    diversity for, 153

Mental health initiatives, 156–159, 163–165
Mental Health Parity Act, 196
Mental illness:
  and Americans with Disabilities Act, 61
  defining, 15–16
  difficulty with employment due to, 6
  discussing, on social media, ix–x
  faking, 24–27
  including, in mental health awareness efforts, 159
  jobs boards for people with, 202–203
  limited usefulness of EAPs for, 125
  mental health vs., 15–22
  misconceptions about, 5, 23–34
  negative portrayal of, in media, 7
  negative response of coworkers to, 121–122
  not recognizing, in yourself, 13, 18–19
  prevalence of, 16
  trouble holding jobs related to, 56
Mental self-care, 99–100
Millennials, 80, 137
Mindfulness, 98
Misconceptions, about mental health, 23–34
Misinformation, correcting, 32–33

N
NAMI Workplace Mental Health Poll, 83
National Alliance on Mental Illness (NAMI):
  on burnout, 79, 83
  on challenges faced by LGBTQ+ individuals, 151
  as information source, 161
  job board of, 203
  on mental health and work, 12–13
  on prevalence of mental illness, 16
Negative symptoms, 20
Neurodivergent individuals, 87–89

Religious beliefs, 100
Remote work, 90
Resources:
  and accommodations,
    53
  availability of, 65
  compiling lists of,
    160–161
  as inadequate for mental
    illness, 18
  increased providing of,
    197
  noticing a lack of,
    155–156
  offered by companies,
    40–41
  personalized, 197–198
  push for more, 162
Responsibilities, adjusting,
    90
Retaining employees,
    146–148
Retaliation, 63–66, 154

S
Schizophrenia, 126
  author's diagnosis of, ix
  author's experience of,
    6–7
  breakthrough symptoms,
    176

early intervention for,
    20–22
  stereotypes related to, 30
  symptom domains of,
    19–20
Schizophrenic.NYC, 126,
    183
Self-care, 93–105
  to avoid burnout, 81–83
  during burnout, 92
  care teams to
    supplement, 115
  consequences of
    ignoring, 115–116
  defining, 93–96
  education and activities
    to promote, 158–160
  emotional, 98–99
  environmental, 97–98
  as necessity, 27–29
  physical, 96–97
  pillars of, 94
  preventative, 101–105
  professional, 100–101
  social, 100
  spiritual, 100
  and stress, 17
Self-isolation, 84, 100
SHRM, *see* Society for
    Human Resource
    Management

219

221